SNOW WHITE
LIFE ALMOST LOST

Originally published in 1983 as *Schneewittchen*.
Copyright 1983, Kreuz Verlag AG Zurich

Translation © 1986 by Chiron Publications
Library of Congress Catalog Card Number: 86-21635

Book design by Lauretta Akkeron
Printed in the United States of America

Library of Congress Cataloging-in-Publication Data

Seifert, Theodor, 1931-
    Snow White : life almost lost.

    Translation of: Schneewittchen.
    Includes bibliographical references.
    1. Loss (Psychology) 2. Interpersonal relations.
3. Schneewittchen. I. Title.
BF575.D35S4513   1986   155   86-21635
ISBN 0-933029-08-X

CONTENTS

AUTHOR'S PREFACE

TAKE TIME AGAIN quietly, to read a fairy tale. Perhaps you can recall the special mood that always comes over us when fairy tales are read aloud, a mood that affects us entirely differently from listening to a lecture on, for example, a different topic. When fairy tales are read, a deep sense of quiet comes over us. Everyone listens as if under a spell, enchanted, and concentrates in an entirely different manner from when they have to do a difficult task. Everyone feels addressed in his or her innermost being.

In earlier times, the teller of fairy tales was a welcome guest in the village. This welcome certainly was not due only to the absence then of radio or TV. Fairy tales simply appeal to us differently. You owe it to yourself to allow yourself this special experience once again.

You might proceed this way. First of all, read the fairy tale that you will find preceding the Introduction to this volume. Then, before you begin to read the discussion, take time to let the fairy tale work on you. Follow the response it creates in you, let the fairy tale's peculiar power and vision enchant you, let yourself be surprised by your own reactions.

The scholarly study of fairy tales has long shown the direct relation of these special stories to human experience and to the human soul. In their means of portrayal fairy tales are naturally colored by the cultures in which they are set. Nevertheless, fairy tales as a genre concern themselves with the great themes and motifs of human experience; for example, the difficult quest for the precious treasure, the three sons and daughters, renewal of life threatened by the death of a sick old king, or the particularly important theme of the animal that comes to aid the hero in his decisive tests and battles.

Fairy tales reflect typical, generally human situations and fates. All readers can rediscover themselves in fairy tales in one way or another. In spite of the "fabulous" transformations, parallels to personal life situations can easily be found, even in fairy tales that initially seem utterly foreign. Fairy tales, then, do not depict individual life histories or experiences; rather, these life experience can be fitted effortlessly into the structure of fairy tales. Following the researches of Carl Gustav Jung, the world-famous Swiss psychotherapist and psychiatrist, psychology holds the view that the fairy tale as a whole reflects the development of the soul of early human beings. Everything that is unique to the individual can be discovered again in this generally human context. The study and interpretation of fairy tales, as they are offered in this series, provides a very important means of access to deeply human concerns.

Fairy tales offer advice and solutions for the most varied difficulties and situations in life. Because they do not express the personal intention of a given author, we may trust them to orient us. It must be noted that critical research has raised valid doubt about the extent to which the Brothers Grimm, whose texts we follow extensively in this series, actually presented the original narratives without substantially altering them. Nevertheless, comparative research has substantiated that the basic structure of fairy tales is always recognizable and that fairy tales from widely differing cultures share many features in common.

You can find examples of how the message and the advice can be coaxed out of fairy tales in the books of Marie-Louise von Franz, Sibylle Birkhäuser, Hans Dieckmann, and Verena Kast. These authors represent a viewpoint to which this author subscribes.

Fairy tales present images of the soul. For this reason it is to be recommended that when reading a fairy tale you not give yourself over to immediate critical reflection. Do not allow yourself to be irritated by seemingly "impossible" absurdities—for example, the transformation of a frog into a prince in "The Frog King." Rather, open yourself again to the world of these images and give yourself over to their effect on you. They speak for themselves, and they speak to us in a different manner from the language of science or mathematics. Moreover, pictures say more than do a thousand words. Everybody understands without difficulty when a person's character is compared with a reed swaying in the breeze, especially if the comment is added that he trims his sails according to the wind. Even to begin to "translate" these images into discursive language would require many lines.

In this sense, fairy tales are images that say a great deal on many levels. Today we know that our orientation in life depends on the world of images. The structure of our brain enables us to comprehend and process information and experience in this way. Complex scientific interconnections are likewise often expressed in images to facilitate understanding. Many times illustrative images express far more than do numerical tables. If, for example, we wanted to express in words the meaning of the traffic signs and warnings that appear along our roads and highways, the results would be most cumbersome. Images have their legitimate place in our world; they are irreplaceable and we cannot do without them.

These few viewpoints are intended to give access to the great world of fairy tales, a world that is enriching in so many respects. Even though I give you further references to literature that you can use to orient yourself cognitively, the most important thing is for you to encounter the fairy tale openly and directly. Then you will find the treasure you are seeking.

Some References to the Literature:

I have followed the fairy-tale texts as given in *Kinder- und Hausmärchen. Gesammelt durch die Brüder Grimm* (Manesse Verlag).

If you want to delve further into this theme, I recommend the following books:

Birkhäuser-Oer, Sibylle. *Die Mutter im Märchen*. Stuttgart: 1976.

Dieckmann, Hans. 1986. *Twice-Told Tales: The Psychological Use of Fairy Tales*. Wilmette, Ill.: Chiron Publications.

von Franz, Marie-Louise. *The Feminine in Fairy Tales*.

Kast, Verena. 1981. *Wege aus Angst und Symbiose im Märchen*. Olten.

These works treat additional major life themes that could not be dealt with in our series. Above and beyond this, they contain important supplementary material that facilitates personal deepening and enrichment through the experiences of fairy tales.

Theodor Seifert

"SNOW WHITE"

ONCE UPON A TIME in the middle of winter, snow-flakes were falling like feathers from heaven; a queen was sitting at a window that had a frame of black ebony, and she was sewing. As she sewed and looked up at the snow, she pricked her finger with the needle, and three drops of blood fell in the snow. Because the red against the white snow looked so beautiful, she thought to herself, "If only I had a child whose skin was as white as snow, whose cheeks and lips were as red as blood, and whose hair was as black as the ebony wood of the window frame." Soon afterwards she gave birth to a daughter whose skin was as white as snow, whose cheeks and lips were as red as blood, and whose hair was as black as ebony wood, and thus she was called Snow White. But when the child was born, the queen died.

After a year the king took another wife. She was a beautiful woman, but proud and arrogant, and she could not stand to let anyone exceed her in beauty. She had a marvelous mirror; whenever she stepped before it and gazed at herself, she said:

Mirror, mirror, here I stand.
Who is the fairest in all the land?

And the mirror replied:

O Queen, you are the fairest in all the land.

Then she was satisfied, for she knew that the mirror told the truth.

But Snow White was growing up and becoming more and more beautiful. When she was seven years old, she was as beautiful as the clear day and more beautiful than the queen herself. Once when the queen asked her mirror,

Mirror, mirror, here I stand.
Who is the fairest in all the land?

it answered her:

Here, O Queen, you are most fair
But Snow White is beyond compare.

The queen was terrified and turned yellow and green with envy. From that hour on, whenever she caught sight of Snow White, her heart turned over in her body, so greatly did she hate the girl. The queen's envy and arrogance grew like a weed in her heart, taller and taller, so that day and night she had no rest.

Then she called a hunter and said, "Take the child out into the forest. I can't stand the sight of her any longer. You are to kill her and bring me her lungs and her liver as proof." The hunter obeyed and took Snow White out into the forest, and when he had drawn his hunting knife and was about to pierce her innocent heart, she began to cry and said, "Oh, dear Hunter, let me live; I will run off into the forest and never ever again come home." Because she was so beautiful, the hunter took pity and said, "Then run, poor child, run." He thought, "Wild animals will soon have devoured you," yet he felt as though a stone had been lifted from

2

his heart because he had not needed to kill her. And when a young boar came running past, he struck it down, cut out the lungs and the liver, and took them back to the queen as proof. The cook had to cook them in salt, and the spiteful woman ate them and believed that she had eaten Snow White's lungs and liver.

Now the poor child was utterly alone in the great forest. She became so frightened that she looked at every leaf on every tree and had no idea how to help herself. Then she began to run, and she ran over sharp stones and through thorns, and all the wild animals raced past her, but they did not harm her. She ran as long as her feet could move, until it was about to get dark; then she saw a little house and went in to rest. In the little house everything was small, but so delicate and so tidy that words can't describe it. There stood a little table with a white tablecloth and seven little plates, every little plate with its little spoon, seven little knives and forks, and seven little cups. Along the wall, seven little beds stood side by side with snow-white coverlets over them. Snow White, because she was so hungry and so thirsty, ate a bit of vegetables and bread from each plate and drank a drop of wine from each little cup, for she didn't want to take all of anyone's food. Then, because she was so tired, she lay down in a little bed, but at first none suited her. The first was too long, the next too short, and so on, until finally the seventh was right, and she stayed in it, entrusted herself to God, and fell asleep.

When it had gotten all dark, the masters of the little house came home; they were the seven dwarfs who dig in the mountains for ore. They lit a little lamp, and when it was bright in the little house, they saw that someone had been there, for things were not so tidy as they had left them. The first said, "Who sat on my little chair?" The second said, "Who ate from my little plate?" The third said, "Who nibbled on my little piece of bread?" The fourth said, "Who ate some of my little vegetables?" The fifth said, "Who picked up something with my little fork?" The sixth said, "Who cut something with my little knife?" The seventh said, "Who drank out of my little cup?" Then the first one looked about and saw that there was a little wrinkle on his bed, and he said, "Who got in my bed?" The others came running and cried out, "Somebody lay in my bed, too!" But when he looked at his bed, the seventh saw Snow White, who was lying there sleeping. Now he called the others, and they came running up, shouting in amazement, and they took their seven little lamps and shone them on Snow White. "Oh, my goodness," they cried, "how beautiful that girl is!" And so great was their joy that they did not awaken her but let her sleep on in the little bed. The seventh dwarf, however, slept with his companions, an hour with each one, until the night was over.

When it was morning, Snow White awoke, and when she saw the seven dwarfs, she was frightened. But they were friendly and asked, "What is your name?" "I am Snow White," she answered. "How did you get to our house?" the dwarfs asked. Then she told them that her stepmother had wanted to have her killed, but the hunter had let her live, and she had run the entire day until finally she had found their little house. The dwarfs spoke, "If you will mind our household, and cook, and make the beds, and do laundry, and sew and knit, and if you will keep everything neat and tidy, then you can stay with us, and you will lack nothing." "Yes," said Snow White, "I'd love to," and she stayed with them. She kept their house in order: in the mornings they went into the mountains and looked for ore and gold, and in the evenings when they came back, their supper was ready. The girl was alone the whole day. The good little dwarfs warned her and said, "Watch out for your stepmother. She will soon know that you are here; don't let anybody in."

But after she believed she had eaten Snow White's lungs and liver, the queen thought nothing other than that she was again the first and the most beautiful, and so she stepped up to her mirror and said:

Mirror, mirror, here I stand,
Who is the fairest in all the land?

And the mirror answered:

Here, O Queen, you are most fair,
But over the mountains where she's gone to stay,
With the seven dwarfs far, far away,
Snow White is beyond compare.

Then she was shocked, for she knew that the mirror spoke no falsehoods, and she saw that the hunter had betrayed her and that Snow White was still alive. And she pondered and she mused again how she could kill Snow White, for her envy gave her no rest so long as she, the queen, was not the most beautiful in the entire land. When she had finally thought out something, she colored her face and dressed like an old peddler woman so that she was totally unrecognizable. In this disguise she crossed the seven mountains to the house of the seven dwarfs, knocked on the door, and called, "Nice things. Cheap! Cheap!" Snow White looked out the window and called, "Good day, dear woman, what do you have to sell?" "Good wares, nice wares," she answered. "Bodice laces of all colors," and brought one made of colorful silk. "I can let this honest woman in," Snow White thought, and she unbolted the door and bought herself the pretty bodice lace. "Child," the old woman said, "how you look! Come, I will lace up your bodice properly for once." Snow White had no suspicion; she stood and let the old woman lace her up, but the old woman laced so fast and so tight that Snow White lost her breath and fell down as if dead. "Now you were the most beautiful," the old woman said, and she hurried away.

Not long afterward, when it was evening, the seven dwarfs came home, but how horrified they were when they saw their dear Snow White lying on the ground, neither moving nor stirring, as if she were dead. They lifted her up, and because they saw that she was tightly laced, they cut the laces in two. Then she began to breathe a bit, and little by little she came to life. When the dwarfs heard what had happened, they said, "The old peddler woman was nobody else but the godless queen. Be on your guard and don't let a single soul in when we are not with you."

But when the evil woman got home, she went to the mirror and asked:

Mirror, mirror, here I stand,
Who is the fairest in all the land?

6

And the mirror answered as usual:

> Here, O Queen, you are most fair,
> But Snow White is beyond compare.

When she heard that, she was so terrified that all her blood rushed to her heart, for she saw that Snow White had come to life again. "But now," she said, "I will think up something that shall destroy you," and with witch's arts, which she understood, she made a poisoned comb. Then she disguised herself and took the appearance of a different old woman. Thus she went across the seven mountains to the house of the seven dwarfs, knocked on their door, and called: "Nice things. Cheap! Cheap!" Snow White peered out and said, "Just go on, I must not let anyone come in." "But you must at least be allowed to take a look," the old woman said, and she pulled out the poisoned comb and held it up.

The child liked it so well that she let herself be fooled and opened the door. When they had agreed on the purchase, the old woman said, "Now just let me comb your hair right for once." Poor Snow White had no idea, and let the old woman have her way, but scarcely had she stuck the comb in Snow White's hair than the poison began to work, and the girl fell senseless to the ground. "You raving beauty," the evil old woman said, "now you're finished," and she left. Luckily it was soon evening and time for the seven dwarfs to come home. When they saw Snow White lying there as if dead, they immediately suspected her stepmother, so they searched and found the poisoned comb. Scarcely had they pulled it out of her hair than Snow White came to and told them what had happened. They warned her once again to be on her guard and to open the door to nobody.

The queen took her place at home before her mirror and said:

Mirror, mirror, here I stand,
Who is the fairest in all the land?

And the mirror answered as previously:

Here, O Queen, you are most fair,
But Snow White is beyond compare.

When she heard the mirror speak, she shook and trembled with anger. "Snow White shall die," she cried, "even if it should cost me my life." Then she went to a completely isolated, lonely room where nobody ever came, and there she made a poisonous apple. On the outside it looked beautiful, white with red cheeks, so that everybody who saw it would want it, but whoever ate a piece of it would die. When the apple was ready, she colored her face and disguised herself as a peasant woman, and like this she crossed the seven mountains to the house of the seven dwarfs. When she knocked, Snow White stuck her head out the window and said, "I mustn't let anybody in, the seven dwarfs have forbidden it." "That's fine with me," the peasant woman answered. "I just want to get rid of my apples. There, I'll give you one as a present." "No," said Snow White, "I can't take anything." "Are you afraid of poison?" the old woman asked. "Look, I'll cut the apple in two; you eat the red half, and I'll eat the white." But the apple was so cleverly made that only the red half was poisoned. Snow White coveted the beautiful apple, and when she saw the peasant woman eating some of it, she couldn't resist any longer, so she stretched out her hand and took the poisoned half. But scarcely did she have a bite of it in her mouth than she fell down dead on the ground. The queen looked at her with horrible eyes and laughed uproariously and said, "As white as snow, as red as blood, as black as ebony wood! This time the dwarfs cannot waken you again." When she was home, she asked the mirror:

Mirror, mirror, here I stand,
Who is the fairest in all the land?

Finally it answered:

O Queen, you are the fairest in the land.

And at that her envious heart was at peace, insofar as an envious heart can ever be at peace.

When they got home at nightfall, the dwarfs found Snow White lying on the ground, and she was not breathing. She was dead. They lifted her up, looked to see if they could find anything poisoned, loosened her bodice laces, combed her hair, washed her with water and with wines, but nothing helped. The dear child was dead, and dead she remained. They lay her on a bier, and all seven of them sat down around it and mourned, and they cried for three whole days. Then they were going to bury Snow White, but she still looked so fresh and alive, and she still had her beautiful red cheeks. They said, "We can't lower her into the black earth," and they had a transparent coffin made of glass so that she could be seen from all sides, and they put her in it and wrote her name on it in golden letters, adding that she was a king's daughter. Then they placed the coffin on the mountain, and one of them always remained with it and watched over it. The animals came, too, and mourned Snow White, first an owl, then a raven, lastly a dove.

Now Snow White lay a long time in the coffin and did not rot, but rather looked as though she were sleeping, for she was still as white as snow, as red as blood, and as black as ebony wood. But it happened that a king's son came into the forest and arrived at the dwarfs' house, there to spend the night. On the mountain he saw the coffin and beautiful Snow White in it, and he read what was written on it in golden letters. Then he said to the dwarfs, "Let me have the coffin; I will give you whatever you want." But the dwarfs answered, "We wouldn't give it up for all the gold in the world." Then he said, "Then give it to me, because I cannot live without looking at Snow White; I will honor and cherish her as my most beloved." As he spoke, the good dwarfs took pity on him and gave him the coffin. The king's son had his servants carry it away on their shoulders. But then it happened that they stumbled over a bush, and the jolt knocked the poisonous bite of apple that Snow White had bitten off out of her throat. Then it wasn't long until she opened her eyes, lifted the lid of the coffin, and sat up and was alive again. "Oh, God, where am I?" she cried. Joyfully, the king's son said, "You are with me," and he told her what had happened, and said, "I love you more than everything else in the world. Come with me to my father's castle, and you shall be my wife." Snow White loved him and went with him, and arrangements were made for a splendid and magnificent wedding.

But Snow White's godless stepmother was also invited to the feast. When she had dressed herself in beautiful clothes, she stepped before the mirror and said:

Mirror, mirror, here I stand,
Who is the fairest in all the land?

The mirror answered:

Here, O Queen, you are most fair,
But the young queen
Is a thousandfold beyond compare.

Then the evil woman uttered a curse, and she became so terrified she didn't know what to do. At first she didn't want to go to the wedding at all, but then she couldn't get it out of her mind: She had to go and see the young queen. When she walked in, she recognized Snow White and was so horrified and afraid that she couldn't move. But iron slippers had already been set over the coals of the fire, and somebody carried them in with tongs and placed them before her. Then she had to step into the red-hot shoes and dance until she fell dead to the floor.

INTRODUCTION

LIFE THAT WAS almost lost—with these words we can paraphrase the theme of the fairy tale "Snow White." Many fairy tales are concerned with this theme to some degree, but here it is a central issue that everyone who reflects and enters the feeling level can sense within themselves. In psychotherapy sessions it is a daily experience that persons report feeling "as if dead," that generally or at certain times—in their sexual encounters, for instance—they no longer feel anything at all. Life seems to stand still. Horrified, many persons see in retrospect that life has passed them by, that they have missed out, that they have remained onlookers and spectators. They admonish, even implore, their sons and daughters to do it differently. A woman who at the age of forty first discovers the vitality she can feel in the loving embrace of a man suddenly sees her past life with entirely different eyes. It seems to her as though she were awaking from the sleep of years, like Sleeping Beauty, or as if a numbness, a spasm, were dissolving, which up until now had blocked and crippled her.

This is where the story of "Snow White" begins. In detail and in the language of images unique to it, the fairy tale describes events that can, without difficulty, be related to such personal experiences. The central question to which "Snow White" seeks and finds an an-

13

swer is: "How do I win back the life I thought I had lost?" Many personal situations can be seen and understood from within this general framework. The answers, as they are given in the text, are likewise so general that readers can easily enlarge and complete them with their own concerns.

CHAPTER I
In the Middle of Winter:
Numb Hearts and the Hope for
a New Beginning

Once upon a time in the middle of winter, snowflakes were falling like feathers from heaven.

THE FAIRY TALE BEGINS in winter, in a cold and gloomy time. Try to imagine a winter landscape: snow-covered trees and fields, cold, icy winds, deep snow on streets and sidewalks. When the snow is deep, moving is difficult, taking a great deal of effort. If people are not to freeze, they must dress adequately for the low temperature. These kinds of images also express something of our soul, and we often use an image to say how we are feeling. We speak, perhaps, about storms of feeling that rage in us; something flashes through us like a bolt of lightning; a hot, burning love or an abyss of emotion moves us. These spontaneous examples show the frequent parallelism or analogy between the world of our souls and the world of things about us.

The introductory image leads directly to the central question of this fairy tale: Can my benumbed feelings come to life again? Is everything over, as I often think

15

it is? Is there for me, too, a new beginning, although I feel as if I'm dead?

Pictures reminiscent of Christmas cards surge up along with such images of a winter landscape: Somewhere in the snowy landscape there stands a cozy little house, light shining from its windows; we think of a warm, homey room, a crackling fire in the fireplace. This is exactly the issue: Images of ice and snow, of wintry rigidity, are closely united with images that protect and sustain life. To them belongs warmth, a great deal of warmth, from the very beginning. Either literally or metaphorically, no warm-blooded creature —neither animal nor child nor adult—can survive without a warm nest. It is precisely for this reason that we refer to the mother hen that takes her chicks under her wing. Young, new life needs warmth. This is true, too, for new beginnings in the inner life, beginnings that over the course of years become necessary again and again.

Each of us commands enough imagination to conjure up images of a winter landscape in our mind's eye to see nature stiff with ice and snow, and to know from our experience that in a few months this landscape will begin to blossom again. "Snow White" begins in just such a condition of lifelessness and colorlessness, of short days and long nights, indeed, of death. We know that no life can maintain itself in snow and ice. Animals and plants hibernate by going under the earth. If snow and ice covered them forever, they could not survive. We know this from those regions of our earth that are realms of eternal ice. Human beings can survive there thanks only to special protective

16

measures. Reports of experiences from research stations in the Arctic emphasize the extraordinary psychic and physical stresses to which the human organism is exposed there. Warmth has a life-sustaining function. If we also consider how difficult it would be to bear the loneliness and the solitude in those long, dark nights without the warming hand of another human being, then the survival value of the warmth of one's fellow creatures becomes very clear.

So the fairy tale depicts a condition that really lives only on hope, perhaps from warming images from the past or from scarcely dared vistas of the future. Everything is dark, nowhere does a light shine, a low point of immobility has been reached. Feelings that were originally warm, perhaps even hot, have congealed. In relationships an icy silence reigns; there is an icy coldness of feelings. Without belaboring the point, we describe phases in a relationship and people we know in just this way. Whenever someone's reaction is "ice cold," we know what is meant, although there has been no drop in temperature to register on a thermometer. Nevertheless, such people seem to us "ice cold" and we even experience their glances as equally chilling.

But since the fairy tale speaks not of ice but rather of winter and at the same time emphasizes the middle of winter, it points to a possible turning point. Our ancestors celebrated the winter solstice; we still rejoice in the lighting of the lights at Advent and at Christmas. Our soul has a deep need, especially in times of darkness, to see a new light, at least symbolically. Jörg Zink entitled one of his books *The Middle of the Night Is the*

Beginning of Day (Die Mitte der Nacht ist der Anfang des Tages).[1] He relates an experience that is difficult to convey in words: the premonition that things cannot and also must not continue as they are at the moment. Admittedly, many people have these realizations again and again but stop short of actually changing their lives. Let us ask the fairy tale how we can deal with such dismal and seemingly hopeless situations in our own lives.

CHAPTER II
Snowflakes in Winter: Small, Scarcely Perceptible Feelings and Hopes

Snowflakes were falling like feathers from heaven.

T HAT IS A VERY DELICATE and almost insignificant image of movement in this rigid landscape. At first it could appear as though the snowflakes only increased winter's power, but that they fall like feathers and from heaven adds two perspectives that point beyond winter. Before you read further, imagine feathers of this kind. Notice what memory images arise and what thoughts cluster around "feathers." Here it is especially important to pay attention to your feelings and moods. Usually feathers awaken pleasant memories and feelings. They are light, soft, delicate; they nestle against the skin; in our feather beds they make us cuddly and warm; they never hurt us. The bird's coat of feathers, the feathers in the hen's wing that protect her chicks, the proud feathers of the eagle that spreads its wings, the feathers in the Indian chief's bonnet, or the feather we want to stick in our hat—all might occur to you. In many respects, the feather symbolizes positive conditions and moods. Nothing seems to be lighter than a feather: "light as a feather" is the lightest we can imagine. The wind can play with feathers, blow them before it and whirl them about.

This image of feathers blowing in the wind is the central motif in the Brothers Grimms' tale "The Three Feathers."[2] In it an aging, weakened king was pondering the end of his life. He did not know which of his sons should inherit his realm, so he told them, "Go forth, and whoever brings me the finest carpet shall be king after my death." To make sure that there would be no argument among them, he led them out of his castle, blew three feathers into the air, and said, "As they fly, so shall you set forth." The three brothers followed the feathers, and the story takes its course. The youngest, whose feather fell straight to earth, ultimately inherits the realm. "And he ruled wisely for a long time," because the feather had shown him the way.

Is it not often small, seemingly, insignificant things that are decisive and that point out the way? In a melancholy situation perhaps a friendly word that was not even intended changes the situation. Or quite unexpectedly meeting a person may call forth a feeling in us that gives our life a new direction. Intended or unintended, it is the scarcely perceptible that here takes on greater significance in the shape of a feather. In the fairy tale of Snow White, the image of the feather functions predominantly as a hint, and the course of the story will confirm what is shown here in so insignificant a form. It belongs to the contradictory facts of life that precisely that to which we grant no importance can attain great significance. The New Testament tells us that the stone that the builders rejected becomes the cornerstone. The insignificant, the seemingly powerless, can overpower the powerful, as so many powerless acts have demonstrated.

The dove, symbolizing peace the world over, likewise wears a coat of feathers. Thus feathers are also a characteristic of birds, often representing them, even if they are not visible. For many people, birds are associated with the free play of fantasy and thought, indeed, with freedom itself. If they could choose freely what animal they would like to be, many people would be birds. As a reason for their choice, they speak of the freedom and ability to fly, soaring unfettered in the skies. If the fairy tale speaks of feathers in the very first line, this is a hint that by looking and listening for the soft, scarcely detectable and seemingly insignificant feelings, images, and impulses that arise in our souls, we may find the beginnings of a change. This free play of forces is largely independent of our thinking and our willing, and hence at first glance it often appears unreasonable, ignorant of the world, or simply impossible. But just when a completely petrified situation in life must be overcome, we need impulses that lie totally outside the rigid system. An idea that is "beside the point" can hint at the desperately needed new element. It has to be beside the point, or it would offer no helpful new insight.

We are not accustomed to paying attention to this side of the soul; the noise of collective convictions and opinions generally considered to be "right" intrude on us all too frequently. We subject our lives to these external standards, but when these standards have lived out their usefulness and no longer embrace life, we find ourselves in a rigid and cold condition. Then it is often only these gentle, "feather-light" intimations of our own soul that can lead us further, even if we are not able at the moment to see where the path goes. In such gray, mid-winter situations in life we should first of all—trustingly—yield to the play of fantasy, to the play of inner images, regardless of where they may lead us.

Also, although it is obvious, the fairy tale expressly mentions that the snow flakes fall *from heaven.* So we should also bear this image in mind too. The sky has always been the realm that carries our expectations and hopes for the future and for countless ages the gods have dwelt there. From the sky the sun warms our earth—indeed it is the realm of brightness and distance. As an image from the soul, it points to a new, expanded consciousness, a new attitude toward life. Such a play of fantasy represents a first, new step toward broadening life. As we examine unconscious processes of development more closely, we can confirm again and again that the unconscious—or, more exactly, the Self—in humans holds in readiness a multitude of possibilities for life and reveals them step by step. It always begins very simply. As in the world of nature around us, so also in our inner nature. Can one word, then, be so important? It can be as significant as the feather!

The initial scene of "Snow White" sets us in the midst of a completely natural event and offers the consolation that even gloomy phases, perhaps even the valley of the shadow of death, can be integrated into a

22

larger, more encompassing cycle. Almost all fairy tales offer hope.

In nature winter is not final, but rather it is a necessary phase in the round of the seasons. The darkest clouds do pass over. This motif of dying and becoming we have yet to encounter in "Snow White," but it is already hinted at in the first sentences. Even developments that we encumber with the weighty name of "rebirth" begin very simply; every plant begins with a first leaf, every new beginning with its first step.

CHAPTER III
Only a Queen . . . : Constrictions and Biases

A queen was sitting at a window that had a frame of black ebony, and she was sewing.

IN MANY FAIRY TALES the king plays a major role in the initial situation. In "Snow White" it is a queen, a woman. Therefore the question of masculinity and femininity is obviously posed more directly than in almost all other fairy tales. Yet, independent of gender, the king and the queen play very special roles in the imagination of their people. They are authority figures, set apart; the individual looks to them for direction. Though we live in a democracy today, we still know very well the significance of monarchy. Stories about the lives of nobility and royalty fill many newspapers whose level of appeal we like to criticize. Nevertheless these newspapers have large circulation. Obviously, royal personages still remain highly significant in modern times. The broadcast of a royal wedding attracts millions all over the world to the TV screen. Throughout history the king and the queen have represented the ruling principle, the norms according to which a state is governed. Their word has absolute authority, their judgment annihilates, their favor exalts

25

their subjects. They are the bearers of powers from which people lived, powers our ancestors believed to be divine. People depended upon kings as upon gods. In European history a king was a king "by the grace of God"; and we still associate kingship with divine sanction, though such power often had tragic consequences through its arbitrary abuse.

In earlier times a king was permitted to exercise his regency only so long as his vitality was unbroken. Among many early peoples the institution of the year-king served repeatedly to demonstrate his power — each year the king had to prove his authority in tests of strength. If the king had become weak and impotent, he could no longer guarantee the continued life of his people, life that was closely bound to his vitality.

Seen psychologically, kings and queens represent the dominant opinions and principles of our personal life, the highest religious, political, or scientific concepts, the rules to which we submit automatically, the guiding ideas according to which we lead our lives, the fundamental feelings that shape it. As an answer to the question "Why?" one is often told "on principle." Children are punished "on principle," although parents sense that their misdeeds do not warrant denying them their supper. "On principle" the slightest fib is punished, even when one knows that it is a case of a child with a rich imagination telling stories. In the process not only fantasy is punished, but the children themselves become "bad," and their inner world is thereby often literally "handed over to the devil." For who leads one into lying, if not Old Harry? Where, up until then, creative fantasy and play enriched young lives, now anxiety, inhibition, and other signs of disturbed behavior take their place. The petrification begins; no more feathers are visible, no path nor goal can be found. Though important ideas and values can be found hidden in each principle—all moral commandments are ultimately indebted to them—the problem begins where a unique personal life is completely subjugated to such general principles, and thereby often almost annihilated. Then we no longer say that somebody judges fairly or is punctual or exact, but rather that the person is a fanatic when it comes to justice or is pedantic and is hard to live with. No living father sits on the other side of the table, but rather a personification of "the principle," whatever it may be. "You eat what's on your plate." These are our kings and queens in good and evil form. By believing she always has to be just, many a mother has at least restrained her spontaneous warmth and love toward her children. Many children suffer under this "justice."

In fairy tales the king and queen often turn out to be old, ill, or doomed to death; even Snow White's mother dies when she is born. The old passes away, the new comes. As a rule fairy tales refer to such situations of change, of transition, and of renewal, and thereby hold answers that can bring about vitally necessary and life-renewing changes in seemingly hopeless situations.

As already mentioned, in our fairy tale the queen appears entirely alone. Here both the king—the masculine principle—and children—the vision of and path to the future—are absent. The image of the lonely queen intensifies the picture of wintry numbness. Life has become one-sided, it has lost its variety, it has solidified into routine. Perhaps it also carries the imprint of a dominant complex, maybe of inferiority or of meaninglessness or of a feeling of impotence. Complexes can rule one's life just as can specific norms and principles. Each everyday situation can, according to cherished expectations, reconfirm a sense of one's own guilt of inferiority. Every criticism from outside is interpreted to confirm one's low worth and to justify practiced reserve. Finally, one resolves not to reveal to the world one's own inability more clearly.

One dominant figure without an opposite and counterpoise, a woman without a man, a man without a woman, very easily falls victim to the tyranny of pet ideas and ruling concepts. In fairy tales this sort of condition is represented, without exception, as needing renewal. Since the psyche talks about itself in the fairy tales that reflect the soul, we deduce from this that holding fast to old ways leads to numbness and to death. The soul needs continual renewal, or at least replenishment. Without transformation and change there is no progress. Vitality withers. The conscious inclination, usually with the strong support of society, to stay in solidified roles is a common problem. Thus, for example, the structure of work is *solely* determined by economic considerations. Today, however, the economy does not exist for the purpose of making human life easier—perhaps it was originally intended to do so—but instead people must adjust themselves to the economy to guarantee that the economic machine runs without friction. However, there are many indications that only a profound renewal, a new spirit, can deliver the individual as well as the collective from the petrifaction that means death, the final end.

Fortunately, living systems—and the human being as an organism is a living system—develop powers that, again and again, point beyond themselves, that slowly or often very suddenly break through existing limits. At first it looks like chaos, yet we can learn to discern the beginnings of order in these conditions that are completely obscure for the time being. We like to lament the collapse of old structures; however, life on earth has always grown beyond them to find new forms. There is always a way forward, none back, for such processes are not reversible.

Referred to the development of a woman, the absence of the king suggests the necessity for a spiritual expansion and renewal. Many housewives and mothers know this problem all too well, but so do many women in jobs that do not suit them. Related to the development of the male, we see here before us the type of man identified with a feminine attitude, a man who possibly has not yet, in spite of his age, separated from his mother and her demands or from guilt feelings related to mother and family. Psychotherapeutic experience also shows that these problems do not automatically resolve themselves as one grows older. Even if their mothers have died years before, middle-aged men can remain frozen in boyish attitudes of adaptation and obedience that have become sterile. Such a man transfers his image of mother over to his wife or mate. Her principles continue to rule, and the man is neither autonomous nor authentic; that is, he has not become himself. In one short dream image a dreamer —a man in his mid-forties—saw his mother as if through a church window, a view that dramatically and pointedly illustrated his still idealizing her and his own constricted point of view. Unconsciously he revered his mother almost as a saint. Along with this he took her word to have absolute validity. He responded unquestioningly with acceptance and obedience, to every stirring of maternal displeasure. Such men, ones held captive by the queen, may be friendly and courteous, but they are not creative. Made numb by such a hardened, narrow femininity, women may have the feeling of having failed in life, of having squandered their time on cooking and children. Not infrequently these attitudes toward life in men and women are linked with neurotic or psychosomatic disturbances and ailments. These deep-seated crises of identity and maturity can, to be sure, lead to new possibilities. However, these crises can lead just as easily to a final rigidity and to further illnesses. The images of the fairy tale do not gloss over these possibilities. In this sense fairy tales are nothing less than "fabulous." They paint vivid, realistic, and brutal pictures; in every age we must plumb their meaning anew. The questions they address are of a generally human kind, as are the solutions they offer. Let us again ask our fairy tale how, in such a constricted situation, things could move forward.

CHAPTER IV
A Window Framed in Black:
The View from Mourning

T HE FIRST SENTENCE of the fairy tale tells us that the queen is sitting at a window that has a frame made of black ebony; she is sewing. Naturally the queen could have sat somewhere else, but the fairy tale seats her just at this place, which grants her a distant, broad vista. That is obviously the first, necessary step, small but unavoidable. Complaints frequently heard are "I can't see beyond it" or "I feel as if I'm up against a wall and I can't see anything at all." Readers will undoubtedly remember having uttered similar statements. In each one of us there lives just such a lonely queen. Following the image in the fairy tale, we can imagine how she raises her eyes and lets them roam over the expanse the window reveals to her.

Follow her example and raise your eyes, look into the distance, and notice what happens in your soul. You can understand this quite literally: Once again let your eyes roam over meadows and fields and wander along the horizon without looking for anything in particular. Do memories emerge, either beautiful or painful? Do longings again come to life or dreams of the loss of long-cherished goals or significant people? We must take care not to dismiss immediately the images of longing, the memories or hopes, as childlike and unrealistic. To do so would put a premature end to the play of these forces on the basis of our partial theories, our limited views of life, glimpsed as if through peepholes. In place of living, creative imaginal forces there arise dry, theoretical concepts or lifeless moral precepts with which more often than we want to admit we can do nothing. The unmediated life of the soul takes place in just such small acts, whether we call them feelings, images, or wishful thinking.

The window implies that a view beyond the momentarily established limits is possible in every situation. We can see beyond the walls of our present situation and place in life, even beyond our inner prison. The thing, really the only thing, we have to do is raise our eyes and look again. We must emphatically encourage ourselves, our mate, or our friend to do this. Unfortunately the impulse to look is often crippled by many disappointments and by sadness. "I don't want to," we then say. Perhaps there is a boundary, a limit to how much disappointment one can endure before finally cutting oneself off and becoming incapable of looking into the distance, but this limit is seldom reached. Dreams and fantasies—the truly vital elements in the psyche—prove this. Careful observations reveal that the unconscious seeks paths in the imaginal language of dreams, and that steps are intimated. Admittedly, we may need an encouraging companion in order to dare to take the necessary steps, and this, by the way, is a central element in personal psychological hygiene.

Every window reveals only part of what lies outside. If the window faces west, we do not know what is happening in the east; if it faces south, the north is hidden. Naturally we can always want more, but here the wisdom of the fairy tale says, "Be satisfied for now with *this* segment; it is the right one for the moment." To generalize, we can really understand people only if we see their segment of the world and if we can feel how the world looks through their eyes, indeed, how it must look. If they are oriented to the west, we know —even if our friends do not—that the sun rises only in the east and that light returns in the east, though initially the view is turned toward the west, toward twilight and night. We must first of all follow their line of sight so that "the darkness" lies before us, the night side of life. It is difficult to bear. Often people need courageous company for a long time until wounds are healed and disappointments are worked through. Only then can "the sun rise again," the new viewpoint be gained.

The burdens can go back years, usually decades. Wounds sustained in childhood are deep, the pain of them seems to be unbearable. Yet, nevertheless, what the child has suffered, the adult is better able to endure, even if it hurts. Sooner or later each of us recognizes that we always see only a small segment of the infinity of the world. That, too, gives us the hope to continue, but it also makes us humble and tolerant because we remain conscious of these limits. Different parts of the world lead to different images of the world. We suffer not so much from the world as it is but rather from our ideas about it, ideas that we have formed on the basis of our personal experiences.

The window, the fairy tale tells us further, has a

frame of black ebony. This introduces us to a material and a color that will appear again later in the queen's wishful fantasies for the longed-for child. Black corresponds to the initial situation in the depth of winter. It cannot get blacker than black. The segment of life that has been accessible to me up until now has a very dark frame: there appears to be no exit, not even a bright spot. Involuntarily we are reminded of the black border on mourning cards, which announces the dark night of loss and suffering. The fairy tale convincingly unites the dark and the light, the narrow and the wide, the mourning and the vision beyond mourning. In analytical psychotherapy we speak of "uniting symbols" through which the soul can find pathways where consciously we see only irreconcilable opposites. Here it is not so much a question of an exclusive either-or but rather of the unifying both-and, doing or seeing the one and dropping or denying the other. This unifying psychic function can be found in the life of every human being. We incline toward thrusting aside the one or the other, toward excluding it from life, not wanting to admit it, yet the soul seeks a path toward wholeness, which, step by step, embraces more, both darkness and light. When related to each other, both have value and meaning. Through crises, suffering, and difficulties—although not only through them alone—we grow.

The frame of the window is made of wood, not of iron or copper, which would also be possible. Wood is a product of the earth, it is a natural material, it is not imperishable, and it has its place in the natural order. Our points of view, including our dark and pessimistic ones, have developed as we have grown and only appear to limit the segment of life accessible to us and lived by us. These limits are a part of it, even if they are hard to bear. Darkness, suffering—should we avoid them at all costs? Throughout the ages we have been told that wanting to eradicate all suffering and all limitation is a desire for selfish superiority. Do we want to be like God, resplendently omnipotent? Surely we must also learn to accept the dark frame around our lives, to own what we have inherited from our ancestors, whether this inheritance pleases us or not. In the events of our personal lives each of us can look back on weavings of fate that make us anything but happy. There are literally centers of gravity where many energies flow together, focal points that bind and limit so long as the energies are not separated out from this amalgam. The fairy tale indicates to us that we are looking at an initial stage, and because it is a beginning, it is also and unavoidably a transition.

CHAPTER V
The Queen Was Sewing: The Hint of Something New

TRADITIONALLY, SEWING has been regarded as a woman's occupation. Since this activity corresponds to old role models, young women today often reject sewing, as it no longer fits their self-image in their search for what constitutes their femininity. However, fairy tales are indeed shaped by social and cultural facts that make use of scenes like that of the queen sewing, but it is more in keeping with their meaning to place them in large symbolic contexts. Even today, however, a glance at the daily activities of many women is still revealing: even if a young woman has never before sewn or knitted, she may feel the impulse to do so during a pregnancy. It gives her personal satisfaction to make something for her own child, and in so doing she creates a relationship with her child. When she sews something, it often relates to an approaching event, even if in the near future.

What seems yet more important in the fairy tale is that the queen was active; she did not fold her hands in her lap. In connection with the initial situation in the fairy tale it seems to me that this merits the greater significance.

In depressive periods, even the smallest activities are important, as slipping into complete passivity and indifference is destructive to the organism. Even if the activities—in our case, sewing—appear insignificant to a critical eye, they serve to maintain mobility and the capacity for change. Even the compulsive monotony of certain kinds of work, like knitting, is better than complete apathy. Here we do not mean to deny that there are illnesses in which the patient wastes away in complete indifference, but even for them the doctor will try repeatedly to move them to undertake even the smallest activity—yes, *move* them—and will view any return to greater activity, however limited it may be—as a success. The queen sewed. She was still active and, we may assume, goal-oriented. She certainly had an idea of what should come of her work.

Many women speak of the contemplative, introspective nature of these activities. While so engaged, they can pursue their thoughts and fantasies, for example, occupy themselves with the child growing in their bodies or with their friend for whom they are making something. It is striking how often young girls knit mittens or a sweater for their beloved, and while doing this they are occupied with all those things that are so new and fascinating in their lives.

In the human imagination it has always been the spinning women who spin the thread of fate—a term still used today—and hence lay down the web of this life and its pattern. Likewise, the spinning women know when the thread ends. Life often hangs on only one thread; if it breaks. . . . Sewing, weaving, spinning are all activities that transcend empirical social questions and role problems of the sexes. For ages past they have been bound up with 'life' and with 'fate.'

Consequently we can also assume that the queen still had some vitality, that she still had a feel for her life. Expressing general human experience, the fairy tale, gives a corresponding piece of advice for such a situation: remain active and involved, be it on the smallest and most modest scale. Regardless how much we resolve to take them, big steps are seldom possible in any event; our good intentions usually end in disappointment. Since small and seemingly ordinary steps are part of "life" and intrinsic to it, "ordinary" carries with it no negative judgment. Let us say it another time: if once again we set about perceiving and feeling into the vital impulses that move our souls, we need an attitude that goes beyond good and evil. Critical judgments that classify things in terms of a known system of norms and values usually mean the end for this timid new life in the soul.

CHAPTER VI
The Prick of the Needle: The Call of Life

As she sewed and looked up at the snow, she pricked her finger with the needle, and three drops of blood fell in the snow.

WHILE THE QUEEN WAS SEWING, during the quiet hours of activity just described, suddenly something unexpected and painful happened. It was not foreseeable, but rather happened quite suddenly. The queen pricked her finger, one of the most sensitive parts of the body. The situation is now becoming critical, and the story takes an entirely new, unexpected turn.

If sometime you give yourself over entirely to the free play of inner forces, of feelings and images, you will observe that suddenly something flashes through you. It penetrates you like the prick of a needle, and you pause at a memory or an image. Unexpected things, things long forgotten, come to the surface and will not leave you alone. Suddenly you know that you are touching an important inner matter. Perhaps you have encountered what psychologists call "unfinished business." An insight or a realization that you have attempted to evade for years may force itself upon you anew. A needle is something quite specific and pointed; it pricks a definite place, and there you feel the pain. The growth that will resolve and overcome the coldness and the lack of feeling begins in a very specific situation. Everybody knows such painful places, ones that have been numb for years. Personal development stopped there, a long time ago. Perhaps initial sexual experiences were so discouraging that a door slammed closed that even today hasn't opened again. Though occasionally one was able to "warm to it" again—language points to the chilling—one lacked strength, courage, or the opportunity to go further. Precisely in regard to new sexual experiences, social and moral boundaries are drawn very narrowly, even now in our own day. However, this is only an example. There are many other places that hurt like needle pricks when we again open ourselves to them and the pain they carry. Deep hurts inflicted by parents-in-law or the husband's relatives in the same house at the start of a marriage can petrify the heart and make the body freeze so that the feeling for one's own value and usefulness noticeably diminishes.

As we know from symbolism in general and from clinical experience in particular, the needle can also be understood as a phallic symbol, that is, in the broadest sense of the word as something masculine. Here it is not a question in the narrower sense of the penis—which would make it a sexual question, which, of course, is entirely possible—but more generally of a degree of potency, of a possibility full of power, ultimately of something fructifying. We know that decisive realizations can be very painful and that the unconscious, as one says, puts its finger on the sore spot. For a woman this can mean that there develops a new, fructifying idea that she should follow up. A resigned man, paralyzed in a negative routine of feelings, may suddenly experience a new, activating impulse. "Finally I've got to do something again; I have to get out of the old rut; I've felt for a long time that I can't continue like this 'til I'm sixty-five." Sexuality expresses a lot of strength and vitality.

We know the special sensitivity of our hands and fingers. Second only to the brain, they are the most "human" organs and symbolize differentiated, sensitive action. Prick, needle, finger—these point to new activities, not only to painful insights, but also to joy. Here we must bear in mind that this pricking happens unintentionally, it simply happens and cannot be undone. Whenever we really deal with the snow, the shroud of our life, and persist in this experience despite all our pain, then this pricking can happen. Then the creative impulse from within one's own soul appears. Then perhaps we have a dream, a fantasy, that reenergizes us, we hear a call that excites us, we encounter a book or a person or whatever it may be. Suddenly we experience the first stirrings of new strength. It's so easy to write "shroud of life" to designate the cold blanket under which our feelings for each other lie, at best lukewarm. Perhaps we should not be so anxious about the chance of "burning" our fingers or our mouth. Our language contains many allusions to the warmth and the chill between people. Yet once life is opened up again, we are confronted with alternatives that can demand disagreeable and difficult decisions. Should I let

43

myself get into a new relationship? Old feelings of resignation ("It's all meaningless and doesn't make any difference any way") may easily push us to a half-hearted decision. We know very well that many marriages are begun in just this way. Also, our own past, with all its sins of omission and its disappointments, can overwhelm us and reinforce our fear of the future. For good reasons we tend to repress all the great hurts and wounds of our childhood. But when we do this, much warmth of heart and feeling is extinguished. Nothing really touches us any longer. We are indifferent to a multitude of oppressive feelings until we feel just that needle prick that embodies the new call to take a chance at a new beginning. This is how the fairy tale tells it, passing on to us the old experiences of humanity.

CHAPTER VII
Three Drops of Blood in the Snow: The Great Conflict

THE LINE OF ACTIVITY hinted at in the needle prick continues in threes. Three drops of blood fall to the ground. According to ancient tradition, three is an active, masculine number. Here it implies that life is not over, that energies still available press both for expression and for shaping. Moreover, given that physical health is relatively intact there are no age limits for this development. Activity and the future are not the prerogative of youth alone. To follow one of Martin Luther's precepts, even if one knows that one could die tomorrow, one should still plant an apple tree today. Even psychotherapists are increasingly freeing themselves from the rigid rule that people are responsive to psychotherapy only up to the fortieth year of life. Only in the second half of life, which we enter about age thirty-five or forty, do we gradually learn to live with our death, which, as is well known, is one of the major well-springs of wisdom. The Psalms admonish us to "take heed of your end and become wise." In response to Carlos Castenada's asking why he should think about his death, Don Juan told him it was "very simply . . . because the thought of death is the only thing that tames our spirit."[3] Death seems to be the only thing that does not hover about us uselessly but rather lets us act in a meaningfully goal-oriented manner.

We can never know in advance when we will prick ourselves, when the fateful three drops of blood from our finger will fall to the ground. Sometimes one gets a premonition and afterwards says, "I knew all along that something was in the air," but frequently we are surprised and astonished that life should take just this turn and no other. We are especially struck by this today because we live convinced of the rational predictability of the world. However, fairy tales teach us —and thereby hand down to us the experience of our ancestors—that new and creative possibilities simply cannot be determined in advance. Otherwise they would no longer be creative in the true sense because we could derive them from what is already known. Complementing the knowledge of the rational, comprehensible, and explicable world which science studies is the knowledge of the positive significance of the irrational, nonderivative, and unforeseeable: "The spirit bloweth where it listeth."

After the event we think we can explain developments; in spite of this it is difficult or impossible to see the future. It is the classical physics associated with Galileo and Newton that has given many psychologists their model of scientific objectivity. That physics holds a rigorously mechanistic world view in which clearly delimited units exert effects on each other according to equally clear and rigorous laws of independent cause and effect. It was thought that if one knew all these factors, one could, in principle, predict every event in the world. Today the world appears to physicists and to psychologists alike as an endlessly complex web of relationships, both in the realm of matter and in that of living organisms. Even the things of this world—be they living or dead—are thought of as simultaneously dynamic and stable patterns involved in a process of endless change. The relationships among mass, form, and energy have become fluid. The universe is something like a pulsing organism, not a rigid clockwork functioning according to mechanistic laws. Conceiving the world in this fashion, as dynamic process, corresponds also to the feeling for life that underlies the images in fairy tales and in many myths. The Bible tells that the birth of the divine child came to pass "when the time was fulfilled." Here, too, relationships appear to exist and to be introduced which defy more precise description. The ancients already knew about "*chairos*," that special moment in life with fateful significance. In modern times Peter Handke said that in the course of each person's life there comes a moment—a mystical moment—when one can decide absolutely freely, without a push from outside. One knows that if one does this or that, one's life will change. But most people let this moment pass them by. The missed slap in the face of piety once invoked by Hermann Hesse lets this moment pass by. Life is a series of missed opportunities, one says, and sadly adds: "If only I had . . . , then today I would be . . . !" What opportunities are we missing at this very hour of our life?

Blood is a very special liquid, "thicker than water." It is one of humankind's great symbols. Among the holy sacraments, blood is the standard of comparison for

every religious sacrifice, a sign of the deepest bonded-
ness. Think, if you will, of blood friendship and blood
relationship. Think of the deepest feeling of revenge
in the blood feud, of especially hard battles fought
to the last drop of blood, and of the exceptional sacrifice required whenever a blood debt is to be paid.
Examples from many different cultures which reveal
to us the significance of blood in human life could
go on and on. Blood is fascinating, it disgusts, it calls
forth strong-feeling reactions. Blood is fundamentally
bound to life. Often we can save a life with blood
transfusions. Life and blood are simultaneously related
to warmth. In a metaphorical sense blood can "run
cold" when we are "frightened to death." Whenever
warm blood flows, there is life. If blood completely
congeals in the body, no help is possible.

Three drops of blood indicate that life has again begun to flow, even if at first in a primal form that the
ego can only vaguely perceive. Sometimes a pressure,
an inexplicable vital impulse not yet directed to any
goal, may suddenly come to life to cause us great anxiety. Courage is not yet the issue because we simply do
not know where this impulse is driving or leading us.
But we would overtax ourselves if we expected the
first impulse toward a new beginning to appear as a
clear goal for decisive action. The new often appears
only as a heavy, dull energy that we don't know what
to do with. "If only everyone would do what they
wanted. . . ." How often we hear this phrase! One drop
can be enough. Often we need only an image or a feeling, a hint or an inner call, to get life moving again.
Certainly, that kind of inner call must be heard and

carefully considered. How many drops of precious life fall to the ground, how many creative ideas and how much living feeling die away because of not being seen and carefully nurtured? Nevertheless, we must not underestimate the anxiety that is almost always tied to the eruption of new life.

The fairy tale alludes specifically to blood in the snow and thus to a particular sort of polarity. If in the snow we see an image of death, then in the blood we see an image of life. Cold and warm, hidden and self-revealing life meet. Thus opposites develop simultaneously which are the starting point both of conflicts and of energy. In the midst of winter is a condition of low energy, of indolence, of inactivity. "What's the point of anything?" If in such moments new vital energies do appear, say by falling in love with a new person, what do you do then? A new, almost unbearable drama, certainly new energy, develops from the opposition between traditional morals with all their "thou shalts" and "thou shalt nots" and the impulse you now feel. If you suddenly get the fantasy of raising canaries and your spouse speaks against it rationally, with "clever" arguments, in no case does an opposition of blood and snow come to pass. Again and again we see that the way to avoid conflicts is to keep the opposites from developing. The consequence is that no energy develops, either, and all of life becomes rather insipid. But if you let yourself become involved in the play of opposites, very energetic exchanges can take place, exchanges that express both the energy and the separation of two poles.

In all these situations the opposition of blood and

snow manifests itself. Much of the power and energy that arises from this opposition frequently fizzles in fights and explosions. Indeed, the fairy tale seems to gloss over something, for, according to it, the red against the snow looked very beautiful. Perhaps this, too, can be confirmed experientially: We visualize new ideas that enliven us in the brightest colors. But it is precisely here that those around us begin to criticize. Of course the good features are not to be denied. But in addition you need constructive, not destructive, criticism! With the help of constructive criticism, realistic plans and goals can be developed that permit realization of the ideas under existing conditions, conditions that often must also be changed as well. Good criticism does not kill the new, vital impulse but rather assists in understanding it and supports its further development. Instead of saying, "You and your pipe dreams" or "Of course that won't work," people should think and plan together. Often it is also important only to understand the sense of such an impulse and initially not be concerned at all with actualizing it. New, young life is still very vulnerable. Thus new, vital impulses almost without exception lead to opposing views and conflicts, conflicts with existing social rules, the church, or morals as well as other individuals. Out of these conflicts grow the energies necessary for realization, energies that are often not inconsiderable.

CHAPTER VIII
The Child:
Transformation and New Beginning

"If only I had a child whose skin was as white as snow, whose cheeks and lips were as red as blood, and whose hair was as black as the ebony wood of the window frame." Soon afterwards she gave birth to a daughter whose skin was as white as snow, whose cheeks and lips were as red as blood, and whose hair was as black as ebony wood, and thus she was called Snow White. And when the child was born, the queen died.

APPARENTLY WITHOUT REASON, the queen wanted a child characterized by the colors black, white, and red. This again adds to the two colors 'white as snow' and 'red as blood' the third color, *black*, mentioned at the beginning. Here there is perhaps an allusion to a sequence of colors which —thanks to C. G. Jung's *Psychology and Alchemy*[4] (the medieval precursor of chemistry),—we know generally reflects the human process of transformation and development.

We would need an entire book to present fully this fundamental process of transformation and renewal. The condition of winter torpor shows the basic possibility of a "life as if dead." Nothing is moving. The transformative character of life seems to have been lost, choked off by the cold and covered over. Too easily the course of the day from morning to evening hardens into a routine. A frequently heard complaint goes: "It's always the same old thing, it's all so monotonous." But all religions are concerned with the transformation of human beings, with their becoming whole, and ultimately with their perfection. In spite of big words, experienced transformation appears only in the small, everyday things. Here each one of us must find and take the first step on our own. Usually we make the other—our spouse, the children, or our parents—responsible that "things don't go right." For this reason we find in fairy tales the most varied references to activity and independent action, be it at first only the dark urge we sense coming from the unconscious. Transformation and action belong together, and they always begin with small, new impulses.

The alchemists, who did not yet have formulas and abstract scientific models at their disposal, spoke of the transformation of matter in the process of chemical reactions with the help of pictures, which, however, represented the transformation of the inner life rather than the transformation of matter. Prior to the development of the natural sciences, matter and soul were still intimately intertwined for humankind. Even the forests and the clouds were still peopled with hobgoblins, trolls, elves, and spirits who "got into us." We have retained this expression up to the present day, and many emotional conditions cannot be better described. Out of the blackness, the "dark night of the soul" as St. John of the Cross called it,[5] there comes light—which, of course, again denies and covers up the darkness—and the reddening as blood and energy.

Associating the child with the three colors represents, as definitively as one could wish, the rebirth of congealed consciousness and its revivification. The possibilities of a person's transformation out of blackness (the alchemical *negredo*) through the stages of whiteness (*albedo*) and redness (*rubedo*) are alluded to in symbolic form. But the child—which always can be understood in the sense of a new beginning in life —proves to be a specific child who represents new life and meaningful change. Given the initial situation in the fairy tale, this has to be so because—as we ascertained at the beginning—there was not even a king, let alone sons or daughters, present. "Snow White" shows a life situation in which creative life has been completely repressed for years and to a certain extent must start at the beginning again. "If the seed does not fall to the ground and die, it brings forth no fruit." Here it is a question not only of renewal but also of rebirth, a concern attested both in the Christian and many other cultural traditions.

We are accustomed to speak of rebirth only in a religious framework. Such an experience seems to be far removed from daily life, and many people no longer have any living relationship to it at all. Why, then, when it is such a fundamental process and experience? Because transformation and rebirth are such important processes in the meaning of life, in our times especially we cannot do without this perspective:

Rather, we should give it special attention and thought. It is surely an illusion to believe that purely rational decisions can suffice to hold in check chains of events in this world that could lead to possible catastrophes. Today we know, for example, about the detrimental effects of environmental pollution—which affect the highest layers of the atmosphere surrounding our earth. We know that a new war would be insanity, and yet everything seems to continue to move inevitably in this direction. Therefore, with all due respect, we must in the same breath acknowledge the impotence of reason. Because these processes of transformation are so vitally important, we experience them as sacred, and precisely what is sacred merits our special regard: We must not forget it. Every day offers the opportunity for small changes and new impulses, for rebirth. The soul is almost always ready.

In our fairy tale a little daughter is born, a new feminine aspect of the soul. This can be related to the psychology of both the woman and the man. When doing this, I must decide from instance to instance what such a new aspect of the feminine in me or in a person important to me could be. This feminine can have to do, for instance, with the capacity for devotion generally, or in the narrower sense with sexuality, with a feeling of tenderness, or with the courage to see intellectual and rational deliberations also from the viewpoint of feeling and value. The tragic thing about natural scientific research and its findings is that so-called objective facts are not seen in terms of their function and their value. A great horror is associated with the discovery of atomic energy, a horror that only gradually—and hopefully not too late—is revealing its effects. That we know something and are able to do something is only one aspect of such a discovery. We must also ask, "Is it good for us?" However, our decisions are influenced hardly at all by feeling and its warmth. In science, too often wintry cold and rigidity rule.

Finally, however, something transpires in the daughter—as the further course of the fairy tale will show: the conflict between the daughter and the mother, that is, between an old principle restricting consciousness and a new, vital impulse. The fairy tale states that this new impulse is more beautiful, that the daughter goes further and stands closer to wholeness than does the mother who, for her part, however, feels and wants to feel that she is at the absolute pinnacle of her development. This comment is important because in a fairy tale similar to "Snow White," it is not the stepmother but rather the mother herself who is the evil figure set on destroying the daughter. In this negative mother we encounter once again the principle of opposites that was represented by blood and snow: the old, customary, and conventional is always the enemy of the new. The usual form is experienced as completed and right, the new impulse is experienced as threatening and destructive. But how is a new form supposed to develop if the old form is preserved without question in its present, seemingly completed shape? Here one first risks one's personal life and needs the moral courage to look the new in the eye, even if it is initially threatening. Can one really always say unequivocally that a relationship is threatened when the one or the other seeks and finds a new partner? The double formulation of the opposites at the beginning of the fairy tale shows something of the particular drama that characterizes such events in our life. How quickly the defense mechanisms known to and described by psychoanalysis come into play as here shown in the naming of the little daughter: in spite of the three colors mentioned—black, red, and white —she is called "Snow White." Her name mentions only one color. That is unfortunate inasmuch as the new life is now associated immediately with the color of snow, which we have also come to know as the color of death. Does that perhaps mean that the new life is threatened with death from the beginning, since *nomen est omen*? In this choice of name is there not already on the mother's part also the wish to destroy this new life? We know today that children are sent out into life with definite injunctions. For example, clinical experience has shown that very many people carry messages like "don't exist!" or "die again!" These occur not only externally in the family; we continually do that to ourselves. If there were a cemetery for our feelings or for our creative vital impulses that have been killed or have died away again, it would occupy a broad area of our soul. Who can say that this cemetery, this inner desert, does not exist? If we wanted to tend all these graves—so many people are immersed only in their old, never-realized ideas—it would cost us a great part of our energy.

In Snow White we encounter a classic case of denial: We do not want to admit that beside the white— which represents as well innocence, purity, the yet unlived life, and therefore, also, absolute possibility—

there also belong the black and the darkness, the red and the affect, the feeling and the blood. We don't want to experience suffering; we repress intense feelings, deep affects. In our personal life-history, of course, we have many good reasons to explain such behavior. But the fairy tale tells us that there can be no rebirth without these *three* colors; without all three everything must remain sterile. Here psychoanalysts speak of a process of countercathexis, which means that energies are mobilized that hamper precisely what I want to actualize. What was experienced as positive is translated into the negative; what appealed to me now disgusts me. Something of this sort can be seen in the "double white" of the daughter's name. In ourselves we find it difficult to take up a personal guilt. We work hard to convince others of their guilt for our misery. Much acumen is devoted to such proofs, but those are deceptive behaviors. By seeming to establish the other's guilt factually, I secretly pursue the goal of disposing of the responsibility for my life. We can see that this process is a very particular kind of "game." One example of such a game is, "If it weren't for you, I'd certainly feel a lot better. I'm not to blame, you are—or at least the circumstances are."[6] The name "Snow White" seems to imply a principle of double innocence or guiltlessness, which constellates corresponding defense and repression mechanisms of extreme intensity. If we do not accept the transformative process with its other two colors, black and red, what remains for us is a seemingly guiltless mediocrity. And thus we again fall into the hands of a collective principle: What was until now vital and pointed toward the future becomes pervaded with the unidimensionality of what is known, and what presented itself in three colors is reduced to one color. Then everything is again clear, transparent, morally clean, without spot or flaw—but the consequence is that our soul remains in a condition of winter, of snow and ice. Yet another time three drops of blood fruitlessly fell to the ground, for ultimately snow is still more powerful than three drops of blood, be they ever so hot.

I would like to encourage you to think back to the last time in your life when three drops of this vital juice again congealed and froze. Surely you still remember: It feels like a piece of life frozen solid. The life itself has left. We each encounter this common archetypal danger just as we do the corresponding opportunities. In a modified form we will meet this state of affairs later in the glass casket. Though the new life only seems dead, it really is and will remain so for all time if no prince comes to bring it back to life.

CHAPTER IX
The Death of the Queen:
Responsibility and Concern

THE DEATH OF THE QUEEN provides a further allusion to the threat to the new life. Considering a new-born infant's need for help and care, the death of the mother is an especially dangerous event, with immense consequences. In the biological as in the psychological sense we know of the infant's complete dependence on the mother or other caretaking person. Metaphorically it is vitally necessary that the old and the new remain united with each other for a period of time. However, the concise language of the fairy tale aims immediately at the heart of the matter, without respect for the kinds of transitions just mentioned: Wherever new life is growing, what is old or lived-out no longer has any place. To the new belongs the right to exist. Yet even if the goal is clear, the further course of the story itself shows how difficult it can be to break away from old habits and convictions. Relapses are just as numerous as they are dangerous. It is hard to satisfy the high and difficult demand for renewal in the face of an attitude to life that is oriented to other values. Let us remember the environmental debate, the call to reduce consumption and arrive at a more equitable standard of living, the effort to orient ourselves to values other than money, power, and economic growth. It can be really dangerous, however, to do away with an old, developed form, even if ever so constricting, unhealthy, and neurotic, before finding a new perspective, one better able to bear the load. We know those periods in the therapeutic healing process where everything seems possible but really nothing is. In every marriage there are lonely times in which we need not reproaches or a superior, know-it-all attitude but the genuine support and help of a friend. The other must stand by us steadfastly, otherwise what looked like new life turns into a feeble rebellion against the superior strength of convention. Such situations are painful and often seem to offer no way out. Again and again the questions arise: "Should I or shouldn't I?" "What will my parents say?" "I could never talk about that with my mother; she'd throw me out today if she knew." This is how adults talk. Even seeming trivialities like taking a part-time job or signing up for a typing course can run into a spouse's violent rejection: "What do you mean!? You won't get a penny from me!" It takes real fortitude not to let the escape from such an ossified relationship end up in the glass coffin, in the glass showcase of memory. "It would have been so nice; it just wasn't supposed to be."

The time of transition is laborious. We know from the great myths that heroes are always threatened; they often have need of direct divine intervention. Let me only remind you of little Moses in the basket, who was finally taken in by the Pharoah's daughter and was thus saved, or of Romulus and Remus, the legendary founders of Rome, who were nursed by a she-wolf. Accounts of threat to young life are a universal motif in the myths of all peoples, because they reflect what the individual experiences. It is not at all uncommon for a fundamental change to be threatened again and again by retreat or collapse, by discouragement and resignation. Inner voices, conscience, and outer threats can so impede the way that one is sometimes hardly able to go alone. If it is to initiate and facilitate a real change, therapeutic treatment also needs a long time.

We read nothing in the story about the king's concern for his child. If it is difficult under normal circumstances to take good care of oneself, then how much more so in these special situations? Many of us have lost the feel for what is good for us, for how to prosper. We know exactly what others expect of us and what our parents, the church, and relatives believe is good. But we ourselves, the persons most involved —are we still capable of perceiving what serves our life? Here psychology speaks of "ego" as the faculty that perceives, observes, decides, and acts, maintaining itself against other internal voices, voices that in extreme cases can even demand one's own destruction in suicide. But this ego is often too weak really to sustain such periods of change.

Contemporary child-rearing practices do not offer this ego much support. Children are threatened with punishment, compared with each other, and filled full of moral precepts for so long that they become completely convinced of their own worthlessness or even badness. It used to be said that the child's will had to be broken. All too often today we still destroy its sense of worth and with that also its trust of itself, its trust of the Self. This "drama" of the child[7] cannot be over-emphasized. We are still far from respecting the full life of the child. Correspondingly we undervalue and despise both ourselves, especially our tender and warm sides, and also our fellow beings. We never learn to be concerned about ourselves, about our inner child, to care for it. If two such abused children find each other with the love they are capable of, particularly difficult experiences lie in store for them when the inner children come to life and tearfully feel their pain. So much is still undeveloped there. These phases are the true acid tests of a relationship and of love. Can we stand it if our mate changes? Many a grown woman would gladly play with dolls once again, so great is the need of her little girl, but does she dare do it? She will look foolish to herself or she fears that she will be made to look foolish. If nevertheless she does dare to, it is with a thousand excuses. Men with their toy trains may have it somewhat easier, but not much. If the inner children are not permitted to play, the biological children are easily exploited in a similar way. The little girl, the little boy, *must* play with dolls or toy trains or erector sets—and, what is more, they must play gratefully. Nothing good can be said about despising one's inner child. To despise it is to let feeling congeal and freeze, and one becomes estranged from the child within. Despite the fact that each of us has had such bitter experiences, parental irony and scornful devaluation remain common practices in child rearing. The king, the current consciousness, is not concerned about the child's welfare.

CHAPTER X
The New Spouse:
Reestablishing an Old Condition

After a year the king took another wife. She was a beautiful woman, but proud and arrogant, and she could not stand to let anyone exceed her in beauty.

THE KING WAS NOT CONCERNED about his daughter, and there is no mention of his mourning the death of his wife. It appears that after the lapse of a certain period of time, perhaps the so-called year of mourning, he returned to business as usual as if nothing important had taken place. Our sensibility misses the entirely natural reactions. When a phase of life comes to an end—for example, when the children leave home—there begins a time both of reorientation and of mourning. Separation from grown daughters and sons is an unavoidable process, but parents can cause children to suffer from their perpetual direct or indirect demands: "We are so alone, why don't you come by more often?" "You do know how morose Dad is, don't you?" Such demands are surely familiar to most readers. Parents are seldom aware how they exploit their children for the solution of their own problems in living, their own emptiness, boredom, or loneliness. Actually, something new should begin for them, aging parents must find new meaning and activities for their lives, but that is especially difficult if the children have been the only content of their lives. "We lived only for our children." Then the expected gratitude, seemingly justified, is sued for in many ways. If that is the case, then certainly we parents have done too much for our children, more than they needed and wanted. We have actually been looking after ourselves. We *had to* do that to hide the feelings that our own marriage may gradually have been turning into a wasteland. Commonly another child is born late in a marriage for just such a reason!

Another area of life may be taken as an example: The normal course of life demands an almost exclusive orientation to the external world—profession, career, security through income and insurances, social contacts, development of a circle of friends, building a house, or buying a condominium. These are only a few of the many compelling circumstances actually dictated from without, and they demand a predominantly outwardly oriented, extraverted attitude if we are to meet them. But eventually our involvement with them begins to decrease. This has less to do with a natural decline of vital powers than with a spontaneously occurring reorientation of vital energy, of libido. If it is natural and necessary in the first half of life for this energy to be directed outward, so in the second half of life it turns of its own accord to the inner world, to the so-called inner objects. Disruptive mood swings, depressive feelings, the impression of getting nowhere, and increasing meaninglessness are the signs of this shift. They are not indications of illness but rather have the character of a hint and present a challenge. If up until now it had been important to identify with parental roles, now it is time to relinquish them, for the shaping of our own personality approaches us as a demand. We might think: "What have I really done for myself? Have I sacrificed myself only for others, for my profession, for an idea to which I felt obliged? What have I gotten out of it?" These questions also hint that a reorientation is at hand and are not indications of neurotic egotism. At such times thoughts of suicide frequently arise. "Things cannot and shall not continue this way," these thoughts say, but this must not be taken literally and misunderstood. Often quite massive symptoms must arise from the unconscious before consciousness, the ego, understands what the real issue at hand is. Something has already died or should die now, it must "finally be buried, once and for all." Everyone knows how difficult that can be, how long and intensively, for example, we cling to old feelings of guilt that are long since outdated. After years of extraversion, one should follow more one's own life, the hints from one's own soul, and no longer seek orientation outside. What I am worth is no longer my successes or the applause, the agreement of others, but rather my own good or bad feeling about myself.

Making this transition means taking time for reflection, including reflection on death; it means asking oneself what themes, tasks, or wishes have remained open in my life. It also means taking upon myself the mourning and the pain associated with this reflection and this reorientation. In this way the change can and will come about. In the language of the fairy tale, this means that Snow White may take up the role and the development at the king's court that is due her, but initially the story does not take this course. Rather, the solution the king seeks in these difficulties is typical: After a short time, he takes another spouse and thereby conclusively seals the fate of his daughter, his own young feeling.

In such times of transition it seems natural to orient oneself on handy, ready-made concepts rather than waiting for and nurturing the growth from within one's own soul. In a marriage, for example, it is hard not to know what one wants and what one should do while one is still subjected to a mate's continuing demand: "Make up your mind!" Many a man briefly attempts again to make some space in his life for tenderness, to take some time to cultivate relationship. Frequently this happens in a relationship to a girlfriend with whom he secretly spends many hours and perhaps discovers a new world. But then? How does he carry that new, young feeling over into his everyday life? How does he keep it alive in spite of stress and pressure to succeed, in spite of moral condemnation, even from within himself? Often the decisive word is renunciation, in many respects: renunciation of accustomed comforts, of more money, of a certain level of luxury. Only with renunciation might it be possible to freely listen to music with the beloved, to caress her hand. Many men believe they have to offer their woman a certain standard of living, although women again and again credibly reassure them they would be satisfied with much less, that the times of shared difficulty actually were the most beautiful. But men stubbornly hold on to such wrong-headed ideas of having to offer material things. With that they quite reasonably justify their compulsion to work and thereby kill their inner maiden. These men attempt to realize externally, with their mates, what they should do for themselves: give shape to their feminine side. Thus the old principle remains in force, the old or the new and its corresponding queen reigns on, as in "Snow White."

About the new spouse we read that she was proud and arrogant, that nobody was permitted to exceed her in beauty. There is nothing to object to about beauty, not even being "the most beautiful," whatever that might be. But instead of nurturing the newly awakened feeling and correspondingly reshaping the contours of our life, we plunge ourselves into yet more work. Many unhappy love stories lead to the exaggeration of an opposite principle, probably in order to drown out the meaninglessness of life after the death of hope. It is not only men who then work "like crazy." We do not sustain what is in the process of becoming; we do not carry through the conflict that has erupted until it unfolds its new possibilities, as seen in the contrast of snow and blood. If previously we were one-sided—the queen was alone at the beginning of the fairy tale—then we really get one-sided and would stay that way forever if the new queen had her way. Even now we still read nothing of the king; the situation remains unchanged.

CHAPTER XI
"Mirror, Mirror, Here I Stand": Self-Confirmation for Better or Worse

She had a marvelous mirror; whenever she stepped before it and gazed at herself, she said: "Mirror, mirror, here I stand. Who is the fairest in all the land?" And the mirror replied: "O Queen, you are the fairest in all the land." Then she was satisfied, for she knew that the mirror told the truth.

MIRRORS HAVE PLAYED a significant role in everyday life since ancient times. Everybody wants one. It is difficult to bear not being able to look in a mirror and check one's appearance. After all, there might be a stain on one's clothing, a flaw in one's makeup, or a loose lock of hair to mar one's hairdo. While the mirror shows us an objective image of ourselves, it shows us even more, as it also reflects our development. The day comes when we notice the first gray hair, when we see wrinkles where previously our skin was smooth. If the mirror is large enough, it shows our whole figure, how it has changed or how it has deviated from the ideal image we have of ourselves. Does it make any sense to smash the mirror when the image that looks back at us from it no longer pleases us? What do we gain by simply no longer look-ing in the mirror, by denying the image opposite us and no longer taking it into account? Sometimes not looking too closely can be useful and helpful but it is certainly dangerous to avoid on principle the knowl-edge the mirror mediates.

Surely you know people who avoid their reflection in the mirror, who never want to see all of themselves, definitely not nude. The mirror seems to reveal some-thing to them that they do not want to deal with or with which they cannot make friends. I recall a situa-tion in an encounter group where one of the partici-pants discussed this problem. After some preparation and with his consent, I gave him a mirror and asked him to take his time and look at himself. It is difficult to convey in words what took place during the follow-ing minutes of his silent gazing into the mirror. Per-haps it can best be put by saying that after long years of self-estrangement, he tried to make friends with this alter ego, that he now wanted to meet himself lovingly, not with negative criticism.

Intimacy with the image in the mirror image like-wise shows us how we meet ourselves. Do we like ourselves? Do we reject ourselves? Just as some avoid their reflection in panic, others live, as it were, with the mirror, anxiously noting every new wrinkle in their face, every hair out of place. They are driven by the continual worry and care that they are not all right as they are, that they are not acceptable. They believe that they should look entirely different, more beauti-ful, bigger, rounder, lighter, darker, etc. On the other hand Narcissus was so much in love with his reflection

70

in the water that he fell in and drowned. Either way, this perpetual, ardent contemplation of one's own image is a burden, a symptom of other troubles. It is, however, a further indication of the importance of the mirror and its function in our lives.

The mirror plays an important role in many tales, myths, and fairy tales. It can also reveal to us things that can be of great significance for our personal development. To this extent there lies in the fascination with the mirror also a hint of our possible future. To recognize the hint and to liberate it from its frequently neurotic covering is a task that we have to perform, either alone or with professional help. The mirror gives us back our image, and therefore is the decisive means of self-reflection, of pondering what I observe in myself, of what I am. Perhaps the continual search for our mirrored image is an expression of this naturally given capacity for consciousness of self, even if not equally developed in all persons. It is plausible to assume that precisely this capacity was of special significance for survival in the course of human evolution. Whoever could take stock of themselves and reconsider their behavior on the basis of this reflected image was in a favored position to adapt to changed circumstances. Thus in a metaphoric sense the image in the mirror represents the call to transformation. This insight is captured in the realization that from time to time we need to take a look in the mirror; and if we are not ready to do so ourselves, sometimes we should be forced to take a look. Hence the mirror leads us into a very central domain of human life.

According to old tradition, however, it is not only

the objective representation of our appearance that looks back at us from the mirror but also our true self that speaks to us from the mirror. The mirror, so they say, reveals our double, our other side, our shadow, which we do not like to see. For this reason some suggest that we carry mirrors on our back, so as to see what lies behind us, so as to come to terms with it. In the sort of psychotherapy that grew out of psychoanalysis, we first look backward. We attempt to deal with the aspects of our personality that have remained in the dark and have had to be repressed. Our ancestors knew that more appeared in the mirror than what was externally visible. You can verify this yourself by attending to the multitude of feelings and scarcely perceptible personal impulses that awaken if you sometime calmly take a little longer with your image in the mirror. Of course, you would need to take more than just a minute and to repeat it many times. This process has nothing to do with vain self-admiration; it is a way to inquire into and to determine the nature of your self.

In our fairy tale the queen does not look just once into the mirror. Again and again she queries the mirror, in a peculiar form of reflection on herself. She seeks only for confirmation that she is the most beautiful, that in every respect she is completely all right. But what does the mirror reveal to her as time passes? It tells her more than she wanted to know: "Here, O Queen, you are most fair, but Snow White is beyond compare." With this there begins the dynamic and the dramatic development of the fairy tale. The mirror reveals to the queen something new with which she must henceforth concern herself. Her beauty is limited, she counts only "here." She is not criticized by the mirror, but rather relativized. Looking in the mirror had served to validate for the queen that everything was still as it had been, that there was nothing new to unsettle her. This confirms our thesis that maintaining the old condition holds in check the disease that is linked with the call for reorganization. Seen this way, the king has gained nothing through his new spouse. The emergence of something new as suggested at the beginning of the fairy tale had not seemed to continue, at least not visibly. Yet Snow White still lives and grows, and suddenly the initial situation is repeated. Now it is not the needle but the changed image in the mirror that penetrates and arouses the queen.

Repeatedly seeking to be proved the most beautiful is seen often in life. Who doesn't want to live in the best of all possible worlds and have the world remain just as it is? To a certain extent it seems to be very beneficial for development, especially the development of the child, to believe that "I am the best." Mothers quite spontaneously confirm this: "You are my good little baby," or "my darling." Such praise lays a foundation for stable self-confidence, and with this one can later again conquer oneself. But whoever must cling fast throughout life to being "the best" is in reality plagued by deep self-doubts and not convinced of personal worth so that daily validation is needed. These are among the consequences of a pedagogy permeated by so many devaluations.

The mirror tells the truth. For a time it may be all right to be uncritically occupied with oneself, for everyone needs a great deal of validation. Especially

73

following periods of loss of inner assurance as to whether or not the old path is still passable, there is need for such validation and encouragement. However, that this assurance is of doubtful value shows in the question's manifold variations and repetitions: "What I'm doing [or not doing] really is okay, isn't it?" Thus one can again console oneself, for the present at least. . . .

Earlier I referred to *chairos*, the propitious moment that one must not let slip by. Decisive opportunities, too, can return many times, yet our ancestors believed that one should not tempt the gods. In fairy tales there are often three opportunities offered to the hero for proving himself and for fulfilling the task of his life. If he is incapable of finding a solution in the allotted time, he turns to stone, he loses his life. I believe both that there are many such petrified people and institutions and also that certain facets of the personality can rigidify this way, a process that our fairy tale talks about. Being self-conscious and caught up in the quest for recognition and validation of one's own worth, convulsive attempts to surpass others, to outdo them and to stand firm as the smartest, the cleverest, the first in all respects—this is what the fairy tale depicts as *the* central problem. The scene with the mirror is really the central point. The course of life can be decided by the manner in which we deal with this basic need so easily observed in small children: the choice or conflict between petrifaction in perpetual anxiety and desperate attempts to be the most beautiful or desperate questing after expansion and renewal, community with others, and an open future with hope.

CHAPTER XII
"A Thousand Times More Beautiful":
Isolation or Community

*But Snow White was growing up and becoming more
and more beautiful. When she was seven years old,
she was as beautiful as the clear day and more beautiful than the queen herself. Once when the queen asked
her mirror: "Mirror, mirror, here I stand. / Who is
the fairest in all the land?" it answered her: "Here, O
Queen, you are most fair / But Snow White is beyond
compare."*

L OOKING IN THE MIRROR has many functions:
self-observation, self-validation, comparison of
then and now, which is bound up with the discovery of
change, or self-reflection arising from the anxious feeling of perhaps no longer being the first and the best.
Here begins the difficult task of perceiving one's own
image and one's own self without the demand
—in the sense of being competitive—of being
unique, the best, the most outstanding. This is an especially important question because here two principles
meet head on that appear to exclude each other: on
the one hand, each of us is unique, an individual who
has not yet existed previously, clearly different from

all other persons. On the other, however, clearly different does not mean better, more beautiful, ahead of the competition, but rather simply other, unique, "just as I am," clearly differentiated from every other. Precisely when this uniqueness is not combined with haughtiness and pride, community is possible both with other persons and with the newness developing out of one's own soul. But if we base our uniqueness on the devaluation of other persons, we are taking an isolating attitude that destroys community. I am placing myself apart from community with people because I reject being like them and instead want always to be better and more beautiful. This isolation leads to loneliness, then to anxiety, and finally to the ever-greater need to be better and more outstanding. This is a vicious circle that leads to the collapse of healthy, natural, human community. Though uniqueness does not have to lead into such narrowness, at least in our culture children have the following experience from the beginning: their ability, for example to turn somersaults, is at first unique for them. Encounters with other children soon teach them, however, that these other children can do the same thing and possibly even do it better. Immediately the question arises: who can turn the best somersault? Who is the first, the strongest, the best, the favorite? On a car trip who is the first to see the church tower of the home town? On a vacation trip, who is the first to see the ocean? The wish to be the first is born with the child. The drive for validation inherent in this is obviously vitally important, while at the same time overcoming the dependence on such validation is of equally vital importance. From fairy tales we can even deduce the rule that those who come to grief are those who cannot overcome this wish for validation but remain caught in it. I do not want to be misunderstood here: It is not a question of completely renouncing self-validation. Only a few people are really able to do this, and then only in their mature years. Rather, we are talking about *dependency* on such validation, about anchoring one's self-esteem in the judgment of other people instead of in the Self. The queen does not know this sort of trust in the powers of growth and the value of her own soul. Probably she trusts only what is concretely visible and also rationally obvious. She distrusts everything that wants to grow beyond the present condition. Immediate, direct trust of the Self is a precious possession, one that above all others we should endeavor to pass on to our children. Those who are at variance with themselves do not have a good basis for surviving the storms of life. Like easily uprooted trees, they collapse, with nothing to fall back on. These persons encounter their souls with mistrust, always competing with others. What is left for them? The queen symbolizes this condition; the fairy tale depicts it with successful precision.

Envy, hate, arrogance grow taller and taller, like weeds. Every gardener knows that weeds have an overabundance of vitality and easily outgrow cultivated plants, that weeds actually do get "bigger" and thrive "better." If they could talk, they would by all means say of themselves: "I am the biggest and strongest and most beautiful because I cannot bear others next to me as equals." Anxiety belongs as an essential motif to this competitive thrust. The powers of the organism are directed one-sidedly and are misguided in many respects. All psychic energy flows into perpetual rumination about how to look even better or how to chase competitors from the field with still greater assurance. Those are not creative and freeing activities in that everything is bound up in competitive behavior. We get caught in our own net and fall into complete dependency. Ironically the one with whom we compete becomes the yardstick, which indicates both a tragic alienation from the other and a self-alienation in the compulsive competitor. Thus we only seem to recognize ourselves in a mirrored image colored with such strong narcissistic desires. We believe that this is us, but it is not us at all. We encounter this estrangement from our most essential nature, a nature that has been conditioned by anxiety and often by decades of adaptation. It is as if we must not be as we really are.

CHAPTER XIII
In the Wild Forest:
The Secret Life of the Soul

Then she called a hunter and said, "Take the child out into the forest, I can't stand the sight of her any longer. You are to kill her and bring me her lungs and her liver as proof." The hunter obeyed and took Snow White out into the forest, and when he had drawn his hunting knife and was about to pierce her innocent heart, she began to cry and said, "Oh, dear Hunter, let me live; I will run off into the forest and never ever again come home." Because she was so beautiful, the hunter took pity and said, "Then run, poor child, run."

FOR THE QUEEN there was only one thing: the girl's death. Yet it is significant that she did not kill her herself. Every one of us knows exactly how we go about it when we want to benumb or kill our feelings. The evening whiskey, sometimes two or more, is one of the best-known means. In fairy tales killing always means making a pressing psychic content unconscious at all costs: repressing it. Perhaps we think "If only I had never met this person," or "If only I didn't keep having such dumb ideas of wanting to give up everything and starting a new life somewhere else." As far as possible, we undo everything. The intention is unequivocal, yet nevertheless something keeps the queen from simply killing the child, which would be possible without further ado in a fairy tale. She looks for another way that at the same time holds the possibility of surviving. The new life is in great danger but not lost. Thus the queen calls a hunter. She gives another person the task of killing the child. This reveals a distinct ambivalence that we can understand as follows: In principle, returning a psychic content to the unconscious holds the possibility of its return. Sigmund Freud recognized the great significance of this process, which he called "the return of the repressed," a common phenomenon that can be observed again and again in the working out of one's own life. In addition to an ever-so-rejecting and self-destructive consciousness, there are also forces that secretly sustain and promote life.

In families we observe a corresponding phenomenon that also characterizes the entire society: Certain qualities of character are strictly rejected. Perhaps they are reminiscent of a relative who had been experienced negatively. Children with these characteristics are made into black sheep: They can do nothing right, they embody the dark side of the family, usually with consequences ranging from sad to tragic. Every society has its blacks, its Jews, or its scapegoats. They always embody what we do not want to recognize as belonging to ourselves, what breaks through our chimera of being the best and the most beautiful and destroys our idealized self-image. Family research today speaks of "delegation" or "attribution" of such negative characteristics.

A self-concept of being other, bad, not-like-us is imparted to such children. They are made to be outsiders and learn to see themselves no other way. Their self-concept is so negatively stamped by the environment that they view themselves critically and in a rejecting fashion. They are at odds with themselves and are very unhappy.

The fairy tale continues, consistently showing such mechanisms of splitting that usually cause a severely neurotic, faulty development. Both externally and internally these mechanisms take their course according to the same laws and with the same bad consequences. Just as we reject, persecute, torture, or kill Jews, gypsies, or blacks, so too do we treat certain components of our own personalities, though they are precisely the components that could guarantee our future hope and further life and growth. Why are we so fascinated by the rhythmic songs of the blacks? Who does not long for a bit of the movement and freedom that we believe we see in gypsies? They can live out what we must deny ourselves, and for this they must pay. These are, of course, largely unconscious processes that must run their course, yet for this reason they are all the more dangerous because they are not controllable. Not infrequently people hate and destroy precisely what could enrich their lives and make them happy. Why do we deny ourselves happiness and, frankly, focus so much good energy to prevent its realization? These questions reach far into the normative foundations of our culture and into the one-sided, patriarchal god-image of our religion. Nevertheless, the organism, the soul, life find ways that lead onward.

The hunter plays a special role in many fairy tales.

Here I remind you only of Little Red Riding Hood, who is freed from the belly of the wolf by a hunter. The hunter enjoys a special bond with animals, as we know from old stories. He is able to keep company with the soul of the animal in a direct way, he talks with the animals before he kills them and asks their forgiveness for having to slay them. In an Eskimo tale the Mother of Eagles reveals the great eagle ritual, so important for the survival of the tribe, to a hunter because he had dealt especially carefully with an eagle that he had had to shoot. The hunter symbolizes that side in us which is only conditionally hampered by consciousness, by its ego quality, its norms, and its constricted viewpoint. The hunter is still related to the wisdom of nature and the sureness of the instincts. However destructively we behave toward ourselves, images always arise in dreams and fantasies that serve life. We can start with the position that there is an unconscious spirit at work in us which produces the stuff of which our dreams are made. This unconscious spirit makes use of the multifarious symbols that are evident everywhere and whose meaning one must know. It determines the content of dreams and stimulates just those compensatory processes that serve further development; in the instance of illness, those compensatory processes serve to heal. Often it is those thoughts we cannot get rid of; indeed, we think we have finally concluded this or that in our life, and yet the thought won't leave us alone. And why not? "I *do* love my children above everything else, but sometimes I just want to run away." "Sometimes there are such cosmic thoughts running around in me that I'm a total stranger to myself." "Of course I love my husband, yet I still have the feeling that someday someone entirely different will come into my life." Thoughts and feelings like these that we cannot get rid of are symbolized by the figure of the hunter who always appears whenever we attempt to repress an important aspect of our personality. The hunter spares Snow White at her urgent plea and outwits the queen. Perhaps he could have done that spontaneously, too.

Nevertheless, in our fairy tale the hunter appears more closely associated with the queen than with nature or with Snow White. He also cherishes the hope that the wild animals will devour the abandoned girl and relieve him of the burden of having to kill her, but ultimately he omits the decisive act and an animal takes Snow White's place. Contrary to his conscious stance, the hunter obviously must do what he can to give Snow White a chance to live. From this we can infer the demand to pay careful attention to the psychic function represented by the hunter and to grant it its autonomy. We moderns find it very difficult not to subordinate everything to reason and not to examine everything for its usefulness and effectiveness. Rather, it is at first hard for us to let something simply be in its suchness. Feelings are "stupid" feelings; we apologize for our hunches and intuitions that we cannot substantiate logically, and we believe only what we can explain. Our scientifically determined pedagogy contributes to this in a fundamental way. However, even science is beginning to recognize that we must let many natural facts stand as they are, because nature makes more riddles for the spirit than we are capable of solving.

Since time immemorial the liver has been the seat

of the soul. It contains the essence of a living being. Often we believe when we have made a thing our own through reason and "digested" it—as does the queen here—that we also really possess it. But to experience and to suffer something oneself or only to know about something are very different things. Those who have not yet had a child of their own can hardly imagine how they will feel as a mother or father. Only when we find ourselves in a correspondingly demanding life situation do we clearly see the difficulties with which other people have had to battle. Sometimes it is almost impossible to explain to one's mate—who perhaps believes she knows better than oneself—what is taking place inside. The mate has immediately categorized it as: "You and your exaggerated feelings" or has already formed a conclusive judgment about us: "You're just too dumb to do that." What else is left, then, other than offering one's partner statements that he or she can categorize since we can no longer talk about anything really important together? Here, now, it is our inner hunter who instinctively offers phrases that sustain communication but that no longer make possible real understanding. Thus, ultimately we protect ourselves from each other instead of developing intimacy. Even if we attempt to solve decisive questions by an act of force or a special act of will, they emerge again in other contexts: The wife gives the husband an ultimatum; he breaks off his affair and becomes impotent.

For the queen it was a shock when again she consulted her mirror, because she knew full well that its word was true. This time the mirror answers her that

Snow White is a thousand times more beautiful than she. The queen is frightened; she trembles and shakes with anger. We can say that the soul will not give up: Again and again it confronts the narrow-minded and faint-hearted ego, which is tied to its hard and fast rules, with the truth. The soul keeps presenting the question of the larger Self and the greater inner person. We cannot simply evade such a confrontation, and we pay a high price if we deny it. But, meanwhile, what has happened to Snow White?

CHAPTER XIV
With the Dwarfs: Hidden Growth

Then she began to run, and she ran over sharp stones and through thorns, and all the wild animals raced past her, but they did not harm her. She ran as long as her feet could move, until it was about to get dark; then she saw a little house and went in to rest. In the little house everything was small, but so delicate and so tidy that words can't describe it. . . . When it had gotten all dark, the masters of the little house came home; they were the seven dwarfs who dig in the mountains for ore.

A FTER VIOLENT CONFRONTATIONS with others, we are all alone with our feelings. A wild loneliness surrounds us; we do not know where to go; everything is dark. The temptation lies close at hand simply to "let everything lie," to give oneself over passively to despair and hopelessness, and to wait. This is a situation that must be carefully considered. There are two sorts of waiting: lethargy, which pushes the responsibility off on others, and being able to wait until the time is fulfilled. In almost all fairy tales there is need of extensive wandering and the fulfillment of many tasks before the magic spell is lifted and life is rediscovered. Snow White puts all her energy into it; she can do no more, but she *must*. In psychotherapy there is no healing without the active and responsible cooperation of the patient, even if the possibilities open are ever so limited. This time of personal change is not a time of great and easily seen success but rather a time of dogged struggle with destructive forces.

The forest is one of those places where wondrous things take place. There, so our ancestors tell us, dwell elves and fairies, gnomes and little forest people, dwarfs and hobgoblins. It is the home of wild and strange animals, and many a young king has followed a white doe or a unicorn into the deepest forest, there to encounter the decisive situation of his life. In the forest Hansel and Gretel find the witch; Blockhead finds the toad in "The Tale of The Three Feathers." The forest, one of the great symbols of the unconscious soul, conceals in itself many wondrous powers that appear in dream images. Thence Snow White flees. There she meets the dwarfs; there she finds a new activity. Psychologically this means that a warm feeling already known or suspected or a new thought or a quiet longing is again repressed, or we may remain entirely alone with them. The decisive thing is that they are not killed.

In the practice of psychotherapy we always stand in astonishment and with great respect before the fact that life—although it can be severely damaged—simply cannot be killed, so long as death itself has not taken us. The seemingly impossible conditions under which development still takes place are nearly incredible. Considering what people tell me of their lives, what they have endured, and the wounds they have suffered, I often marvel that many people are not even more ill than they are. In situations of absolute loneliness—where we stand before vitally important decisions or where we must come to terms with ourselves—there seems to be, so at least the fairy tale says, one path above all others that remains open: the path inward. In modified form here we experience once again what appeared in the initial situation in the fairy tale, when the queen meditated on the snowflakes that fell like feathers from heaven. This often incomprehensible play of unconscious forces, this attentive listening and the work on one's own soul connected with it is the task that now falls to Snow White.

Now the fairy tale particularly emphasizes the smallness of all things that Snow White finds in the dwelling of the small dwarfs. Admittedly, one of the seven little beds does correspond to her size. Here we meet a pair of opposites, the one pole of which has already concerned us several times: If for the queen everything was in the realm of the superlative, the greatest, the most beautiful, and hence also the most visible and capable of being represented (after all, one wants to show off what is most beautiful, especially to competitors), from now on everything, at least everything that serves further development, happens in secret and in miniature. The real life appears to have withdrawn into the unconscious; on the level of the royal court, on the other hand, hate and splendor continue to rule, as does a seeming calm until the mirror reveals its new truth.

In its language of images the fairy tale points out

both tendencies that meanwhile have become solid resistance and the means for the treatment of neurotic illnesses. Neuroses are the result of years of faulty development in which the child's vitally important and unique needs and peculiarities have either been too strongly inhibited or their expression has been associated with the feeling of being different, of not belonging and of being bad. The need of every living being to show itself to be competent and to be loved because of and despite his or her uniqueness can be demonstrated from the start. Jealousy vis-à-vis a younger sibling belongs here. The evil and destructive cycle begins when the parents to too great an extent deny the child trust and recognition. As with hunger, thirst, and sleeplessness, a condition of deprivation develops and leads to a craving for recognition and validation. In the case of starving persons, if a certain threshold is exceeded, they may take measures that become annoying and that no longer correspond to society's concept of "normal." The word *normal* contains the linguistic root *norm*, standard, rule, guideline. Each new human being is measured and judged by his or her environment. Adults who must always be the center of attention suffer just such a hunger, often for their entire lives. The attempt to satisfy such a hunger becomes a character trait; for example, the "craving for recognition" is self-defeating because everybody withdraws from such persons. If these persons then begin to fight for recognition, they become correspondingly aggressive (in the biological sense it is perfectly consistent and unavoidable that they do so) and become even more unbearable. This natural process is blind and needs eyes, the eyes of a perceiving and alert consciousness, of a mirror. The manner in which the mirror is then dealt with decides the further course of life. In our fairy tale the decisive events happen in the realm of the dwarfs.

At this point I must introduce a new perspective. The old and the new queens, the king, the hunter, the forest and the wild animals, the dwarfs, Snow White, the casket, the prince, as well as the poison of the apple, are imaginal representations of emotional facets or processes in *one* person. Our earlier reflections indirectly pointed to this fact, but it had not been explicitly stated and described. Each one of us contains all these tendencies. If possible, every one of us would like to leave most things as they are ("It's so much more comfortable"), but we would also like to undertake new deeds. The preceding discussion must be integrated into this framework. Thus, in "Snow White" we have before us a typical conflict in which the old and the new, the past and the future, doing nothing, megalomania, and new modesty are all fighting with one another. Old splits, originally created for protection and then consolidated, and a new, more holistic and more complete way of life oppose each other, and it is the search for meaning that is at stake. In medieval tales only after his great quest did the knight really became a man and a knight, the husband of the princess, or the king. Parsifal is a powerful example of this.[8]

Beyond the seven mountains live the dwarfs— small, helpful, often also mischievous, but always creative beings known to us from the stories of our childhood. They still stand in our gardens. In Scandinavia people bring out the trolls in winter and build dwellings for them. We believe they are good house spirits, they watch over the treasures of the earth, they know the secrets of nature. Thus dwarfs generally represent still-unconscious natural forces beyond good and evil to which our ego must find a relationship. The depth to which they point is shown us in the figure of Merlin in the Grail legend. Ultimately the dwarfs are still gods. In antiquity they were the phallic attributes— the little "fingers" (*daktyloi*)—of the great goddess and mother: creative potencies are often expressed in the form of finger and hand. That dwarfs are supposed to serve the totality of the individual and the step-by-step process of becoming whole is shown by the number seven, which since time immemorial has represented totality. The fairy tale even lays special value on repeating this number: seven little plates, seven little cups, seven little beds. It is not easy for Snow White to get herself settled in, and yet it is as if a place for her had been planned, as if she had to come. Friends and lovers often express a similar sense of inevitability that they had been intended for each other from long ago. There is a feeling it is "the way it ought to be," that it "feels right," and that things are "in order." In a very broad sense, the Chinese concept of "being in the Tao" refers to such a state of "harmony" between man and world, god and cosmos, inner and outer nature. Even in our so-damaged world, things would look different if along with—not necessarily instead of—economic and financial considerations there were simultaneously a search for harmony, with nature as a counterforce.

For Snow White as for the dwarfs it is at first a strange meeting, yet they quickly find their way to each other. If we are accustomed to leading our life within the framework of conventional habits of thought and to integrating our relationships into a ready-made system of social rules, then an encounter with the creative powers of the unconscious is at first strange, even shocking. The careful, detailed work that Snow White must do in the dwarfs' house is comparable to what happens in psychoanalysis: Hour by hour we are occupied with images of the soul, we work with our dreams, we attempt to discover the lines of development of our life, we try to find and bear and work on the damaged areas. Whoever has really tried to talk about the soul with a friend or spouse will have noted the sensitive and delicate way we then treat each other. Seemingly little feelings and hurts and hopes enter into our togetherness and shape and form it accordingly. When working with couples I usually have the impression that spouses have never yet talked with each other about the truly important things in their lives. Often we keep silent about the essential thing that moves us. But here the fairy tale gives us courage. Though penetrating to the deeper realms of love and setting aside omnipresent blockages is difficult and requires careful, patient work with one another and sometimes with the help of a trained therapist, it is possible and accessible to everyone. So we also find our way back to that genuine modesty, humility, and tolerance, to the brotherhood that opens hearts and establishes connections. That is the path to eros.

The mirror also conveys this message: Even if you

do not want to admit it, dear Queen, powers live and move in you that are greater and more powerful than you are. These powers also belong to your reflection and are part of your self, of your future personality. Even if in hate and evil intent, the queen nevertheless again sets out to seek Snow White. This reestablishes a connection that appeared completely broken off by the process of repression described earlier. For really the fairy tale could have ended here. Everything is as it always has been, an old principle has been replaced by a new one that is like the old one because it is not creative. What was once so alive in me, my hot longing for life, has again vanished into the unconscious. The split in the personality has been preserved, and the character armor is unaltered. The contents of this consciousness may differ from earlier contents, but its rigidity and repressive structure have remained intact. In this nothing has changed.

CHAPTER XV
Deception and Poison: The Battle for Life, Love, and Death

And she pondered and she mused again how she could kill Snow White, for her envy gave her no rest so long as she, the queen, was not the most beautiful in the entire land. . . . [S]he crossed the seven mountains to the house of the seven dwarfs, knocked on the door, and called, "Nice things. Cheap! Cheap!" Snow White looked out the window. . . . Snow White had no suspicion.

EVEN IF CONSCIOUSNESS and the ego want to preserve themselves, the autonomous dynamics of the psyche and of the self want other things. Disguising herself first as a friendly old woman, then as a peddler woman, and lastly as a peasant woman, the queen now offers Snow White bodice laces, a comb, and an apple. The young girl falls for the deception, though the dwarfs have emphatically warned her, "Watch out for your stepmother. She will soon know that you are here. Don't let anybody in." And the next time they say, "Be on your guard and don't let a single soul in when we are not with you." Certainly it is not always easy to distinguish the voice of spirits from other voices, but who does not know that warning "small voice" from within one's own soul? In the midst of an important conversation I can suddenly sense how sad and depressed I have become, how I begin to become resigned and give in and let something that I do not want to happen to me happen. Very clearly I sense how I "really" should act if I am going to remain true to myself. If I have to accept the consequences of the decision made passively rather than actively, this bad feeling can accompany me over a long period of time. It holds true in small as well as large matters, in daily purchases—I buy something that doesn't quite fit because I felt sorry for the salesclerk—and in decisions as great as having another child despite being forty years old or adopting one. The presence of the dwarfs means that union with the unconscious processes offers protection against such one-sidedness.

There are times when one has to be unreachable. In our intimate relationships, too, we must learn to deal with the fact that for long periods the other person walks a path about which we may not be told, a path one often does not yet understand or which one cannot take in at a glance. Our questions or our doubt itself can be poison for the other. These are often sensitive processes in the other and difficult to perceive. It is not always easy to know when I should leave the other alone or when I should ask questions because the other cannot step over the threshold to engage in a deep mutual discussion. Here very much will depend on agreeing on the signals that we give each other. Then the other knows what role it is permitted to assume at that moment in my life, although it is not necessary to do so. One does not need to be afraid to tell the other: Take some time this evening for me.

Snow White succumbs more than once to the old woman's temptations. The queen's offers refer to vanity, fame, honor, and surpassing beauty, to what is visible externally and to what can be exhibited. Who would not like to impress, not least of all, one's partner? But at the same time it is these instinctive wishes that make us dependent on our surroundings and rob us of our freedom and autonomy. If the only important thing is to show off and prove this or that to other people—ultimately with the intent of telling them how wrong they are, indeed, how impossible they are—then we poison our original feeling just as the old queen attempted to poison Snow White. That is a sure way to the glass coffin for every relationship and for our feelings.

I believe the earnest message of the fairy tale is to be found in this passage. As soon as we have even the faintest hope of becoming important or of outdoing someone else with the help of our new feeling—the new creative impulse—we are already poisoned. How many have not stopped playing a musical instrument they have just taken up because success did not come soon enough! All too easily we imagine how friends will marvel at our skill. . . . In decades-old marriages one sees again and again the same processes: Both believe they cannot do what is really important to them because, of course, of the other. . . . "Of course I would, but my husband would absolutely refuse to go along with it." "What would my wife say about it?" "What would other people say about it?"

Thoughts like this bind us up and suffocate our soul; they poison all spontaneous and creative intuitions just as surely as the comb poisons Snow White. It is precisely emotional spontaneity, warmth, straightforward devotion, the small, uncalculated compliment that must not be infected in this way—"what effect will I have and how will I look?" As we know from the story of Samson and Delilah, our hair symbolically can represent a spiritual power and an ability that only all too easily can be poisoned. Whatever wants to grow also needs introverted quiet in order to mature. Is this necessity perhaps the real heart of our longing for peace and quiet, and is this longing only secondarily the result of external stress? Can we really just let other people find themselves in peace, discover their own style and rhythm?

Even after many years of marriage, going to bed at different times is still a problem for many couples. Every evening they suffer the same irritation: The one has to go now, the other can't go yet. Each always experiences this as a form of a seeming demand; and without exception the mate is accused. We talk only of what the other did to us; we do not talk of our own lack of readiness to risk corresponding conflict and stand up for our own wishes. Ultimately all these posioned thoughts suffocate our soul, just as the bodice laces suffocated Snow White. But too often we do not risk the ultimately freeing conflict, even if it is uncomfortable. If the poison of narcissistic self-display in regard to the free breathing of one's soul and one's thoughts is not bad enough, it becomes absolutely lethal in the realm of relationships, of love, of eros, and of intimacy between man and woman.

When the evil queen came the third time, she offered Snow White the half-poisoned apple she had with her. "Snow White shall die, even if it cost me my life!" she had cried when the mirror drew her attention to Snow White's superior beauty for the third time—note here again the dynamic number three. She trembled and shook with anger. The conflict draws to a head, the either-or of life and death is at hand. Since ancient times, literally since Adam and Eve, the apple has carried great symbolic meaning, and as the love apple it refers for the most part to the relationship between man and woman. But, ultimately, because of its round form it refers symbolically to the human wholeness represented in the union of man and woman. In earlier times the king received the imperial orb, symbolizing the entire land. William Tell's apple still plays an important role in maintaining unity of the Swiss cantons right up to the present, as the apple is an important symbol serving to preserve and maintain Swiss unity. The apple that the queen offered was both white and red. Here the colors of the transformation process appear—again, with the exception of black, which is perhaps contained in the poison. In the apple scene the fairy tale steers toward the dramatic high point; it is literally a question of all or nothing, as we often so casually say. The question of love, of eros, is a life-and-death question. If we have missed this question, then what do all our accomplishments and all our riches mean?

> Love is such a fateful factor in the life of every human being because, more than anything else, it has the power to release the living from their ego-bound consciousness; it brings us a hint of a transcendental happening, making it possible for us to attend a divine play of the union of Shiva and Shakti, god and goddess, beyond the banality of this earthly life. It is a mystery which no human being has so far penetrated but which is at the same time the goal of life, born anew in each of us. All that we can say is that it is part of a process of reciprocal individuation, of becoming conscious and whole in the encounter. . . .
>
> When a man does not awaken to some awareness of the eternal element that is central to love, he may readily make a personal tragedy of it; in that case "a spark of the eternal fire hisses out in a puddle"; the "divine child" of the two transcendental factors, the symbol of completed individuation, cannot be born either. . . . Whoever cannot surrender to the experience has never lived; whoever founders in it has understood nothing.[9]

What poisons our love relationships? The love for another is frequently poisoned in that we really do not intend him at all, but rather need and exploit him only for the purpose of our own self-display. Are we such great guys when we can call a particularly beautiful woman "our own," as they say? Together we eat the apple of love, but with what is the red half—its particularly attractive, feelingful side—poisoned? Or do we cling to the other so that he can no longer move, so that all his wishes to leave such a relationship are accompanied only by guilt feelings? It looks as though even the positive unconscious powers—the dwarfs —could not unconditionally protect us from the poison of power and of negative narcissism. Eros and power are mutually exclusive. "There is no fear in love." Again and again we attempt to get power over the other out of anxiety. A great many marriages are no drama of love but rather are dramas of power without end. The fairy tale points out to us power and self-display as *the* poison which benumbs, which makes us feelingless. Snow White is again as if dead.

Earlier in the book I had mentioned games. Things look as if we really want to talk with our spouse. We begin with a certain self-criticism, an obvious attempt to remove conflict. "I know that I am too easily hurt and too sensitive," etc. Trustingly our spouse agrees with us and relates this or that recent observation that could be taken as very critical. "After all, you brought up the subject." Now comes the decisive point: Every criticism *can* hurt if we let it. If the one criticized now answers, "Well, of course, I'm good for nothing. You told me that clearly enough just now. Really, why do I keep starting such conversations again and again with good intentions when you're only going to cut me to pieces? I know I'm useless and that you only want to criticize me." *That,* then, is the poisoned apple. An offer was made to reestablish the love relationship, but what happened? Death entered. No embrace, no tenderness, no eros in any form, only a cold emptiness, a cold void. Hans Christian Andersen's ice queen reigns again when we offer each other poisoned apples.

CHAPTER XVI
The Glass Coffin: Between Life and Death

W HEN SNOW WHITE had eaten the apple and fallen to the ground apparently dead, the queen cast a horrible look at her, laughed out loud, and said, "As white as snow, as red as blood, as black as ebony wood! This time the dwarfs cannot waken you again." And then when she again questioned her mirror, it finally answered her: "O Queen, you are the fairest in the land." Now her envious heart found peace—or as well as an envious heart can. Cynically and contemptuously she has once again mentioned the colors black, white, red, and, implicitly, the number three. Obviously she has now finally succeeded in putting an end to the new life, symbolized by Snow White, much as one swears never again to let this or that into one's life. Peace has arrived, the peace of death, but love, or eros, has died. We see this when the marriage is glued together again, the relatives are pacified, the son stays home for good and takes over the parents' business, the unmarried daughter quits her job permanently to take care of her ailing parents. Perhaps she shouldn't do it, but isn't that a good deed? Only her soul knows the answer to this, and it speaks to her in images. The soul is her compass.

The fairy tale, too, leaves the question open and confronts us with the image of the girl lying in the glass coffin. The dwarfs cried for three days, a hint that some still-hidden dynamism is yet there.

> Then they were going to bury Snow White, but she still looked so fresh and alive and she still had her beautiful red cheeks. They said, "We can't lower her into the black earth," and they had a transparent coffin made of glass so that she could be seen from all sides, and they put her in it and wrote her name on it in golden letters, adding that she was a king's daughter. Then they placed the coffin on the mountain, and one of them always remained with it and watched over it. The animals came, too, and mourned Snow White, first an owl, than a raven, lastly a dove.

These images show us also that in the unconscious a state of relative peace has arisen that, however, can change in either direction: either toward definitive lowering into the black earth or toward a new vitality. Both remain possible; the situation is still open. Psychologically this also means that on the part of the unconscious an intermediate solution can be accepted for a period of time. For example, one terminates an analysis without the feeling of final closure at the same time in the knowledge that one neither wants to nor should go further just now. The encounter with the forces and demands of one's own depths, especially in regard to the creative life process, is a long and often dangerous path.

The path of individuation, as C.G. Jung called this process, takes place through many such intermediate steps. On the one hand, as demanding in its dynamism and its symptoms of illness as it can be, on the other the unconscious seems very conciliatory again. Here, too, it is the art of the psychotherapist, free from the poisoned hair of his or her own preconceptions or released from suffocating therapeutic ambition, to be able to accompany the patient on the difficult path with poison-free love. Likewise, in marriages there are recurring phases in which both partners simply do not yet know whether they want to bury their relationship forever in the dark earth and set out for new horizons or whether there still are shared chances for them both. These are times of relative calm, also of relative distance and coolness, that must be endured and borne, times during which both partners nevertheless must carefully observe their own unconscious if the glass coffin is not to permanently encase the relationship.

The glass coffin has many levels of meaning. We encounter this motif in many fairy tales, as in the Brother Grimms' "Glass Coffin." This motif also turns up as a glass house or a glass mountain and always refers to two things: to (1) splitting off, accessibility, to not experiencing; and to (2) clarity of vision ("everything is as if behind glass"). Many see their problem clearly, and yet it no longer moves them. They tell the most horrible things from their life, speak of losses, of unfulfilled longings, of broken loves, of the deepest wounds, even of suicide, but they no longer experience any feeling, no affect. It sounds as though their own fate no longer touches them. Glass isolates: We can see our feelings but are no longer moved by them. Hence the glass coffin is a perfect image of a split-off part of the soul, at the time not developed and scarcely alive, about whose existence we have perfect knowledge.

Something more to consider: Snow White is put on display in the glass coffin; that is, the dwarfs do it with her. The theme of self-display—"Look at me! See how beautiful I am in my tragic plight"—appears again. This cannot be otherwise, because the problem is not yet resolved. Unrelated narcissism and the victory over it through becoming enmeshed again in the human community still stand in hostile, mutually exclusive opposition to each other. A living form of meaningful self-display which does not have as its goal the moral annihilation of the other has not yet been found. Fairy tales can end here, too, in the public display of a living corpse. Again and again we incline toward saying what others have done to us instead of doing something about the problem ourselves. We literally sun ourselves in the radiance of our misery and failed life. "Just look, if my father had not forced me to take over the business . . . ." "At bottom my whole life is senseless because . . . ." Complaints, laments, accusations, but nothing else. A glass coffin. Of course the misery of a life that seems failed until now is everywhere apparent; every lineament of being, every posture, even the manner of using one's own time reflect it all too distinctly. It is transparent. Yet what is the poisoned apple here that isn't spit out? What is the secret of our own anguish that we conceal so carefully? What paralyzes us so that we cannot finally get going before it really is too late? Even when it appears that "the old woman" has seemingly been completely victorious over Snow White, there is still a hidden dynamism and

106

a singleness of purpose that is neither so easily nor so quickly discovered. That would be the other significance and possibility of the glass coffin: the call "Seek me! Find me!" I suspect that ultimately, instead of acting, each one of us often goes about sentimentally with a favorite negative feeling, looking in the metaphoric mirror and feeling sorry for ourselves: "Don't I really have it exceptionally hard?" "Can anybody ever be more lonely than I am?" "Nobody will ever understand me!"

The location of the coffin indicates that the fairy tale views the element of being looked for as the more important: "They placed the coffin on the mountain" and the dwarfs watch over it. Thus it is surrounded by creative forces in the soul. The birds—the owl, raven, and dove—represent the two colors black and white and likewise suggest that a further transformation within the individuation process is possible, a possibility that appears in the fairy tale in the person of the prince. What the dwarfs have written on the coffin also points in this direction: "They wrote her name on it in golden letters, adding that she was a king's daughter." These are significant additions.

Mountains represent the highest places in a landscape. You cannot go higher. In analytic treatment this corresponds to a fact that can be observed daily: The unconscious goes from a great distance to meet the conscious ego. The unconscious reaches up, so to speak, as far as it possibly can into consciousness, into the earth, the image of the maternal ground. Signs and symbols point again and again to the issue at stake, the core of the problem. Since in the development of every personality we are dealing with a segment of the path of individuation, the name is always of significance. The dwarfs have inscribed it so that some time someone might read it, if anyone ever came. When do we perceive what the soul says? Our often appearing like an open book captures this experience. It is now the task of consciousness, which in the meantime has also changed: the prince, not the old king, will come to read this inscription and then take the necessary steps. Nature, the organism, the unconscious, can go up to a certain point; then there is need of conscious perception, taking a stand, deciding, and acting. Ultimately evolution did invent the brain too!

This side of the "Seek me! Look at me! Look at my beauty!" reconciles us with ourselves and gives us back the trust in our own worth so that we do not petrify in futile self-display. Then I know my own worth and my own beauty.

The glass coffin seems to me a fitting symbol for the condition of our feelings, our eros, and our relationship to others and to ourselves. Are we still alive? Do we still know of things that were once upon a time? Do we hope for something that perhaps will come again or not but that lies in a glass coffin at this vital moment? We split off what was important, and after the fact we found good reasons for having done so. "You know, you've got to understand that when they keep on saying . . . ."

I believe it is the eros toward the other and toward ourselves that we banish into the glass coffin and view as a museum piece. This is narcissism instead of mature eros. For example, many daughters have been devoured by their mothers. In taking their life histories I always ask about the grandmothers, for they are often more important than their helpless daughters. The mother often poisons the girl's eros during her tender relationship with the father, and the feelings of the son for his wife often remain firmly stuck in the limits set by the mother. Perhaps as a grown man the son still dreams of nightclubs and whorehouses and looks furtively at pornographic magazines. He senses something, but his Snow White lies in the glass coffin. Can he talk about that with his wife? He wouldn't dare; her criticism would be too hard and too cutting. But even in these forms life still reveals itself. Otherwise why would such fantasies be so widespread, even if decadent?

CHAPTER XVII
A King's Son Comes into the Forest:
Encounter, Sacrifice, Treasure

Now Snow White lay a long time in the coffin and did not rot, but rather looked as though she were sleeping, for she was still as white as snow, as red as blood, and as black as ebony wood. But it happened that a king's son came into the forest and arrived at the dwarfs' house, there to spend the night. On the mountain he saw the coffin and beautiful Snow White in it, and he read what was written on it in golden letters. Then he said to the dwarfs, "Let me have the coffin; I will give you whatever you want."

THE INTERVAL, the phase of relative calm, comes to an end. A new impulse awakens. The king's son discovers the coffin on which, written in golden letters, there stands the name of the beautiful girl. Now the prince knows no other goal than winning this maiden. We do not know where the prince comes from. He represents the creative impulses of life arising from initially undetermined realms, impulses that nevertheless often take hold precisely where years ago we gave up. In psychotherapy it is formulated this way: "Then I really have to continue or start again where

I stopped when I was eighteen—or ten,—or three."
C. G. Jung defined neuroses in general as the goal-
directed movement of psychic energy consistently
leading back to those places "where life stopped."
These are facts of experience. We can paraphrase this
idea by saying that further developing what is unfinished, making up deficits, setting aside imbalances,
and taking care of things postponed gives meaningful
shape and form to one's life. Psychologically we speak
of the onset of a regression. During a regression, both
old experiences, early wounds and pain, and also the
possibilities of life blocked years ago, are brought
to life again in the present. This is a process involving
fantasy that abolishes the boundaries of time. It is a
"living past," old experiences are newly enlivened and
become the object of reflection in the present. Old
rigidified structures become flexible again or are
suffused with new life. The exactitude with which
wounded areas are again located is impressive, just as
is the intensity with which each person desires further
development.

In the language of the fairy tale it is usually princes,
youths of royal blood, to whom the role of redeemer
falls. "Sleeping Beauty" depicts this process in classic
form: The prince penetrates the hundred-year-old
thorn hedge. Explaining the concept of kingship in
historical terms, when kings ruled over peoples and
clans the king also carried the image of a high inner
value, the Self. This provided the basis for his actual
power, just as parents likewise carry the projections of
inner guiding structures. In the psychoanalytic sense
the young prince is the future king; that is, his are the

112

soul's new powers that point toward the future, the new enlarged consciousness that is only viable when it unites in actuality with the potential that has ripened in the unconscious. I can be ever so full of longing and warmth and tenderness, but if at the decisive moment of fulfilling encounter I am not ready to act, the drops of blood again freeze in the snow. The significance of the inner encounter and relationship between the ego and the unconscious cannot be emphasized strongly enough.[10] This is the prerequisite for growth and the health of the soul. Disturbances in this relationship, which also embrace the relationship between the ego and the larger Self of humans,[11] are the prerequisite and sustaining factors of emotional troubles (neuroses). Courage, endurance, and the patient support of a friend, spouse, or therapist are necessary for the success of developments that often get under way again only in the later years of life. If it is to be durable, the happy ending to which fairy tales like to refer can be attained only with the greatest effort. The prince offered everything that he had. He invested everything in order to win Snow White, and the dwarfs finally gave him the coffin as a gift. Here we face the paradox that, following our greatest exertion, we get the treasure for free because it cannot be won or gained by working for it. So it is also in love: We must exert ourselves indefatigably, yet it remains a gift. I do not love my wife because she does so much for me, but that she is also there for me is still a part of it. On the other hand, we find ourselves again in the domain of the poisoned apple if we make love dependent on certain behaviors: "If you really loved me you wouldn't be going to the movies without me." "The fact that you sometimes want to take a vacation alone means you don't really love me any more." It is difficult to describe what is meant here, but the old concept of grace fits best. In spite of all our efforts, nothing can be gotten by force: The real thing remains a gift. Neither sacrifice nor action, neither indefatigable exertion nor personal renunciation guarantees "success" in the realm of human relationships. Perhaps only a small word at the right time tips the balance decisively. The text reads further: "But then it happened that they stumbled over a bush, and the jolt knocked the poisonous bite of apple that Snow White had bitten off out of her throat." It is interesting to note, linguistically, that no active verb form is used. The king's son did what stood within his power. For him more than carrying her away was not possible. Although there seemed to be no prospect that Snow White would come back to life, the prince united himself with her. He knew that without her—that is, to begin with, without her image—his life would have no value. "I cannot live without her." Many a reader will have said something like this. All of us have at some time met another toward whom we felt such feelings, when an inner voice clearly said, "I need this person unconditionally." This is the way every love story really begins. Today we are ready to do almost anything to win the beloved, who embodies the incomparable treasure for which no sacrifice seems too great.

The scientific study of couples' relationships and marriages has shown that we see and find in the other exactly what complements our constricted life and

114

makes of it a greater whole. For this reason there arises the feeling of being only "half" when living alone and of being complete only when together with the other. These external phenomena reflect in projected form the corresponding inner events to which this fairy tale refers. The development of personality and individuation takes place, step by step, by means of such experiences. Many people have the good fortune to alter their existing marriages so that both can grow. Others must seek new forms with new partners, though where the path leads cannot be seen in advance. We do not know where we will get to when the wind begins to blow the feathers and we follow them.

One question still remains for our consideration: Would Snow White have become the mature woman —we may assume that she developed in that direction—if she had remained Mama's Snow White at the court, if her mother had not died, if she had not had to experience the malice of the queen? Many fairy tales ask such questions concerning evil. Without witches there would be no heroes, without fire-spewing dragons, no dragon slayers and new rulers. Are they not here as well, the powers that always want evil but create good, as is said of Mephistopheles in *Faust*? This dynamic does not make the evil principle either good itself or only an extreme diminution of the good. Evil remains in principle evil, and it is also subject to judgment according to whether or not it has fulfilled its function as driving force or opposite pole.

Thus the light and the dark aspects of life in their entire dramatic polarity and paradox are intrinsic to our path. In the mirror of the fairy tale we find useful hints as to how to deal with such situations and how not to lose courage. We can also see that the dark phases of a love relationship are part of a greater whole, if we only know how to deal with them. The question of evil in the fairy tale cannot be adequately considered here, however, but there is a good deal of stimulating literature on this theme.[12]

CHAPTER XVIII
"You Are with Me": Rooted in One's Own Earth

Then it wasn't long until she opened her eyes, lifted the lid of the coffin, and sat up and was alive again. "Oh, God, where am I?" she cried. Joyfully, the king's son said, "You are with me."

THE POETRY OF THESE WORDS reveals itself to anyone who is in love and is loved in return. The language of the great feelings is simple: It says everything. Where do I go, if not to you? And where do I live, if not with you? "You are with me" is the answer to all questions, yet we need not listen only to lovers. Is there a more consoling word for a frightened child who believes it is lost? A mother need say nothing more than "I'm here. You're OK now." The world and the soul are again in order and in harmony.

This being present to the beloved is also an inner experience. After long wandering and estrangement I have finally come to myself again. The time of being "beside myself" is past. Words like "contemplation," "knowing oneself," "roots in one's own soil," or "finding oneself" express this inner meeting. The theme of meeting oneself in all its forms—from self-reflection to self-criticism to self-destruction—is of paramount importance to us. Today we are in a position to annihilate ourselves completely, as global self-destruction is an acutely threatening possibility. Will we escape it? I believe that a pointer—such as fairy tales give us and as embodied here in Snow White—can show us alternatives, alternatives that must be chosen by the individual. With the individual begins the transformation that can progress from the one to the many. If we find and honor our own inner earth, the planet earth will also again become something like our mother, which in fact it always has been.

CHAPTER XIX
"She got so Terrified, so Terrified": The Seed of Evil

But Snow White's godless stepmother was also invited to the feast. When she had dressed herself in beautiful clothes, she stepped before the mirror and said: "Mirror, mirror, here I stand, / Who is the fairest in all the land?" The mirror answered: "Here, O Queen, you are most fair, / But the young queen / Is a thousandfold beyond compare." Then the evil woman uttered a curse, and she became so terrified she didn't know what to do.

MANY FAIRY TALES describe both happiness and unhappiness, love and a cruel ending. Usually we like to see only one side, the positive one. The colloquial expression "just like in a fairy tale," describes this very understandable but certainly childish wish: Ultimately everything *has* to turn out well and come to a happy ending. Everybody knows the sadness and disappointment of witnessing a tragic ending. We see the double face of life with reluctance; we do not want to place the dark and dangerous side next to the bright and sunny. But fairy tales always point to both.

In Chapter X, "The New Spouse," we dealt extensively with the queen. Our inclination to seek conventional solutions where a very personal answer is called for and is necessary proved to be a dangerous temptation. Such general answers—what "you" must do or must leave undone "naturally" and "as a matter of course" in this situation—are legion. They are linked with the demand that it "really" ought to happen thus and so, and also with the assurance that everything will go well then. For this reason these collective solutions are dangerous temptations; they relieve individuals of the necessity of seeking and defending *their* individual point of view.

The fairy tale says nothing about what has happened meanwhile with the queen. If we look back once again over Snow White's path, we recognize in her, too, the inclination to fall prey to temptations. The scenes in which she purchased the laces, the comb, and the apple from the old woman, the disguised queen, speak a clear language. While she was with the dwarfs, Snow White was still a long way from staying wholly in touch with herself, perceiving and respecting her personal feelings as the intelligible voice of the Self. Permitting and actively exerting herself in behalf of her own growth and development were still possibilities, just dwarfs. These possibilities were working as creative forces of the unconscious; however, their impulses had to be shaped responsibly by the ego. Snow White was in the process of building a relationship to them. How far did she succeed? That remains the decisive question.

The various figures of a fairy tale can be viewed as graphic representations of processes and events within *one* person. Seen this way, even the queen is a part of the whole person, and indeed the part that obviously has not changed and does not want to change. In the closing scene she quizzes her mirror, which again gives an honest answer, "The young queen is a thousand times more fair." At this point an open situation appears for the last time. Here the queen still has a chance to enter into a relationship with the new and larger part of the soul that is pointing to the future. The old and the new, past and present, could have formed a living union. Certainly, conventional opinions, traditions, and general demands are not to be evaluated only negatively. They are the product of long experience and offer orientation where a personal perspective is still lacking. But if they take predominantly the place of the personal perspective, especially for adults, life as an individual is basically extinguished. Millions of people have no capacity for personal judgment; for example, they have no means to oppose a skillfully presented political ideology. They are and remain parts of a collective.

The queen does not change; she remains as she is. Rather, she utters a curse, and then "she got so terrified, so terrified that she didn't know what to do." This is astonishing. Did she feel her weakness?

All we have today are intimations of what our ancestors knew, what they lived, what they did. Blessing and curse are two tremendously important forms of transmitting a supernatural power, either for good or for ill. In all honesty we must say that nobody knows what powers we summon or call down on a person, but in every instance we have in mind transpersonal and extrahuman powers; whether they are supernatural remains to be seen. The queen's curse means that every step in development, every phase in "you are with me" achieved ever so laboriously, is still threatened by renewed destruction, by powerful energies. Old family traditions to which sons and daughters must submit can be so strong that their new relationships are subject to great stresses. Mothers, particularly those living alone, often demand that their son have lunch with them at least twice a week. In doing this they appeal to the general rules of social ethics, to gratitude, to their loneliness. Only with severe pangs of conscience will such a son reject this demand. Even "unbelievers" cannot burden themselves with a curse. They would rather forsake their own way that does not correspond to mother's ideas, but in doing so they lose their own ground. For our fairy tale this means that Snow White bears the germ of future temptations in herself, and she is susceptible to the collective pull in whatever form it may appear. No meeting of the two elements—stepmother and daughter—takes place; they face each other at a highly charged distance. The conflict can break out again at any time if no transformation takes place. A remnant of possible dynamism is suggested in the twice-mentioned anxiety. Doubled references underline the importance due this situation in the fairy tale.

The queen's anxiety is probably the last stand of the intuition: "Actually I always knew it, but I didn't follow this inner voice. Now it is too late." Then only anxiety is left. Even if in other circumstances this anxiety might still bear the seed of hope, here it is the knowledge of a now inevitable, fateful course. Obviously there is a point in time, differing from individual to individual, after which things take an inevitable course. Old omissions can be made good only to a limited extent. If hearts have finally hardened toward each other, if trust is shattered after literally thousands of disappointed hopes and attempts, then efforts at reconciliation have no chance. What remains would be grace and forgiveness, but who really receives that from others? But even forgiveness and grace undo nothing. The locus of anxiety and one day of the inevitable is where I should have changed because I knew better. To this extent remaining stuck in collective forms and norms against one's better knowledge is a germ of evil. Where is my "Here I stand, I cannot do otherwise" instead of a "What will people think"? The queen represents transformation refused, the archetypal possibility of individuation not lived out.

CHAPTER XX
The Red-Hot Shoes: Collective Cold and Heat

*Then she had to step into the red-hot shoes and dance
until she fell dead to the floor.*

IN THIS BOTH PENETRATING and macabre image
we encounter two forces: the power of fire and the
icy coldness of cruelty. Attributes previously associated with the possessed queen now seem to come also
from the young king and his bride. This refers to a self-
contradictory, paradoxical state of affairs. The destruction of evil corresponds to "common sense"; evil receives its well-earned punishment and dies, vanishes.
But, psychologically, vanishing means that it becomes
unconscious again. Then we fall victim to the illusion
that it is vanquished. That it is *not* vanquished is
shown by the fact that the destruction of the queen op-
erates according to the same principles—thus they
are preserved—which the queen likewise followed in
her murder fantasies toward Snow White. Destruction
fantasies remain destruction fantasies; they cannot be
interpreted away. Under certain conditions an end
may justify such means, but they do not thereby become "good." In "justifying" there is again the process
of ascribing to the good powers what was previously

evil. But the means do not thereby become good. They remain highly doubtful, even if we hope to be able to ascribe positive forces to evil means for good purposes as happens, for instance, in blessing of weapons. At least in this context evil is supposed to become good. Who does not believe the fight is for a good and just cause? In our times even a balance of terror is proclaimed unavoidable. Paradoxically, arms control then appears as "evil," the manufacture of the most horrible explosives appears "good." But in their essence and in their effect these means remain what they always have been: evil.

For thousands of years humanity has been concerned with the question of evil. Though we have found many answers, we have not solved the question. In most recent times C. G. Jung was concerned with these pressing burdens in our life and even reflected on the dark side of God, for example in his book *Answer to Job* (1952).

The intended destruction of evil is but an illusory solution, effective only for a limited period. The opposition of these two primal principles cannot be canceled out, at least not insofar as we can comprehend this field of tension. The encounter with the shadow, the so-humiliating dark side of the personality, remains a task that cannot be completed once and for all. The shadow can contain diverse elements. A few basic guidelines, however, may have general validity. For example, can the torture of human beings or the destruction of our earth ever be viewed as good? In view of the great prevalence of both, the question of coming to terms with evil but not denying or repressing it cannot be ignored. Only solid personal judgment can withstand the collective curses of, for example, ideological misanthropy and invidious enticements to consumerism.

All lovers have experienced something similar. At the moment of meeting a miracle seems to happen: An I and a Thou find each other. Hitherto unexperienced feelings and powers awaken, which all seem to mean one thing: "Thou, the Beloved." However, no one has yet been spared discovering that this great and wondrous personal experience of happiness, of fullness, of I and Thou, of the absolutely unique is only a glimpse in the present moment of the possible future. It is a possibility, far from being an accomplished reality. Years of hard work must follow in order really to obtain this personal experience. If in the end, then, there remain constant bickering, boredom, and a slow death of what was once so much alive, then once again "'a spark from the eternal fire has been hissed out in a puddle.'"[13]

Whenever two people bind themselves to each other, they bring with them the entire burden and possibility of their humanity, in each case shaped by family and national traditions. Both people have their own "evil" within. To the extent they each face themselves openly and honestly, both soon get a chance to feel it. This would then be an additional way of seeing the last scene. The fairy tale "Snow White" ends with the macabre dance in red-hot slippers. Icy cold and incandescent heat, two aspects of powerful affect contained in every love relationship, here stand opposite each other for the last time. The dance until death begins. If these two primal forces cannot be individualized, they can have annihilating effects. In an encounter begun in ardent love, ice-cold calculation and glowing hate can quickly become irreconcilable opposites in a relationship that is still entirely collective, hardly individual at all. Divorces, too, are then an illusory solution. Unless they signify the beginning of a process of personal transformation, divorces only push aside the evil or leave it at blaming one another. The path to truly personal feeling is, unfortunately, long and arduous. This fairy tale makes that clear.

So as not to sketch only the "grand" contours, let us mention an excerpt from the daily life in a marriage. Again and again the couple find themselves in heated arguments because the husband persists in wearing wrinkled sweaters. The wife cannot bear it if his clothing does not conform to her perfect sense of order. "What will people think of me if I let you run around looking like that!" In fact, she is ready to sacrifice the relationship to principles of order and cleanliness which are so important to her and which she sees as having nothing to do with her personal feelings for her husband and their love for each other. Nevertheless, her desire to save their relationship prompted their coming for a consultation.

We always move in the field of tension between a joyous dance of life and a dance to the death. May we dance the one with each other, growing all the while, and not forget the other as a possibility close at hand?

At this point the fairy tale ends. The new task lying before Snow White and her husband is indicated by the situation just portrayed. Here lies the general meaning that touches us all: our similarity with this fairy-tale couple. The end of a fairy tale is at the same time the beginning of a new phase of development, either for an individual or perhaps for all humanity. It remains open as to how the young king and his spouse will deal with the powers they have encountered in their young lives. Good and evil belong to the wholeness of life, but only in their entirely personal form do they reveal their possibilities. Endless amounts of blood have already flowed in the name of a general good, regardless of how it has been rationalized. Many evil things have happened. The story of Snow White ends with this problem and the demand it poses.

NOTES

1. J. Zink, "Die Mitte der Nacht ist der Anfang des Tages" (Stuttgart, 1970).

2. *Grimms' Tales for Young and Old*, R. Manheim, trans. (Garden City, New York: Anchor Press/Doubleday, 1983), "The Three Feathers," pp. 230–41.

3. C. Castaneda, *A Separate Reality.*

4. C. G. Jung, *Psychology and Alchemy*, in *Collected Works*, vol. 12 (Princeton: Princeton University Press, 1953, 1968).

5. *Johannes vom Kreuz [St. John of the Cross]*, J. Boldt, ed. (Olten: 1980).

6. E. Berne. *Games People Play: The Psychology of Human Relationships* (New York: Grove Press, 1964).

7. Cf. A. Miller, *Prisoners of Childhood* (New York: Basic Books, 1981).

8. See E. Jung and M.-L. von Franz, *The Grail Legend* (New York: Putnam, 1970; reprinted 1986, Sigo Press).

9. M.-L. von Franz, *Projection and Re-Collection in Jungian Psychology* (LaSalle, Ill., and London: Open Court, 1980).

10. C. G. Jung, "The Relations between the Ego and the Unconscious," in *Collected Works*, vol. 7, *Two Essays on Analytical Psychology* (Princeton: Princeton University Press, 1966).

11. T. Seifert, *Lebensperspektiven der Psychologie* (Olten: 1981), esp. ch. 11.

12. See V. Kast & Ingrid Reidel, *Das Böse im Märchen [Evil in Fairy Tales]* (Fellbach: Bonz, 1978); and H. Dieckmann, *Twice-Told Tales: The Psychological Use of Fairy Tales* (Wilmette, Ill.: Chiron Publications, 1986).

13. M.-L. von Franz, *Projection and Re-Collection in Jungian Psychology* (LaSalle, Ill., and London: Open Court, 1980).

DATE DUE

SEP 8 1987	MAR 1 8 1991
MAR 30 1990	NOV 0 5 1990
MAR 1 8 1991	
JAN 1 4 1991	
	MAR 1 3 2002
APR 30 199	DEC 1 7 2004
OCT 2 5 2001	

BRODART, INC.   Cat. No. 23-221